Death of a Salesman

Arthur Miller was born in New York City in 1915. After graduating from the University of Michigan, he began work with the Federal Theatre Project. His first Broadway hit was *All My Sons*, closely followed by *Death of a Salesman*, *The Crucible* and *A View from the Bridge*. His other writing includes *Focus*, a novel; *The Misfits*, first published as a short story, then as a cinema novel; *In Russia*, *In the Country and Chinese Encounters* (all in collaboration with his wife, photographer Inge Morath), and *'Salesman' in Beijing*, non-fiction; and his autobiography, *Timebends*, published in 1987. Among his other plays are: *A Memory of Two Mondays*, *After the Fall*, *Incident at Vichy*, *The Price*, *The Creation of the World and Other Business*, *The American Clock*, *The Ride Down Mt. Morgan*, *The Last Yankee*, *Broken Glass* and *Resurrection Blues*. His novella, *Plain Girl*, was published in 1995 and his second collection of short stories, *Presence*, in 2007. He died in February 2005 aged eighty-nine.

Claire Conceison is Quanta Professor of Chinese Culture and Professor of Theatre Arts at Massachusetts Institute of Technology (MIT). She is a scholar, translator and director whose teaching and research include Chinese theatre, Asian American theatre, play translation and sport as performance. She is author of the book *Significant Other: Staging the American in China* (2004), co-author of late Chinese actor and former cultural minister Ying Ruocheng's autobiography *Voices Carry: Behind Bars and Backstage during China's Revolution and Reform* (2009), and editor of the anthology *I Love XXX and Other Plays* by Meng Jinghui (2017). She wrote the introduction to *'Death of a Salesman' in Beijing* (2015), a new edition of Arthur Miller's 1984 book *'Salesman' in Beijing*, and is a contributor to the volume *Arthur Miller for the Twenty-First Century* (2020). Her articles have appeared in publications such as *American Theatre*, *Asian Theatre Journal*, *Theatre Journal* and *TDR*.

Susan C. W. Abbotson is Professor of English at Rhode Island College, USA, where she mostly teaches dramatic literature. She co-wrote *Understanding Death of a Salesman* with Brenda Murphy (1999), is the author of *Student Companion to Arthur Miller* (2000) and *A Critical Companion to Arthur Miller* (2007), and numerous articles on Arthur Miller. Past President of the Arthur Miller Society, she now manages their website and Facebook page, and was interviewed for their first podcast; she is also the Performance Editor for the *Arthur Miller Journal*. In addition, she has authored *Thematic Guide to Modern Drama* (2003), *Masterpieces of Twentieth Century American Drama* (2005) and *Modern American Drama: Playwriting in the 1950s* (2019). She has published articles on William Inge, Lillian Hellman, Ivo van Hove, Eugene O'Neill, Sam Shepard, Tom Stoppard, Mae West, Thornton Wilder, Tennessee Williams, August Wilson and Paula Vogel in a variety of scholarly books and journals.

Death of a Salesman

ARTHUR MILLER

With commentary and notes by

CLAIRE CONCEISON

Series Editor: Susan C. W. Abbotson

BLOOMSBURY

NEW DELHI • LONDON • OXFORD • NEW YORK • SYDNEY

METHUEN DRAMA
Bloomsbury Publishing India Pvt. Ltd
Second Floor, Building No. 4
DDA Complex LSC, Pocket C – 6 & 7
Vasant Kunj, New Delhi 110070
www.bloomsbury.com

BLOOMSBURY, Methuen Drama India and the Diana
logo are trademarks of Bloomsbury Publishing Plc

First published in India 2023
First published in Great Britain 2022

Cover image: Packed bags (© shaunl / Getty Images)

This edition published with permission from Bloomsbury Publishing Plc,
50 Bedford Square, London, WC1B3DP,UK

A catalogue record for this book is available from the British Library.
A catalog record for this book is available from the Library of Congress.

ISBN: PB: 978-93-5640-424-3

2 4 6 8 10 9 7 5 3 1

For sale in the Indian subcontinent only

Series: Student Editions

Typeset by RefineCatch Limited, Bungay, Suffolk
Printed and bound in India by Thomson Press India Ltd.

To find out more about our authors and books visit www.bloomsbury.com
and sign up for our newsletters

MIX
Paper from responsible sources
FSC® C010615

Contents

Chronology vii

Introduction ix

Historical, social and cultural contexts ix
Genre and themes xi
Play as performance xvi
Production history xviii
Academic debate xxii

Behind the scenes – Chinese actor/translator Ying Ruocheng on working with Miller in Beijing xxv

Further study xxix

DEATH OF A SALESMAN 1

Notes 123

Chronology

1915 Arthur Asher Miller born 17 October in New York City to an upper-middle-class Jewish family in Manhattan.

1928 Bar mitzvah at the Avenue M temple.

1929 Stock-market crash leads to Great Depression, Miller family experiences financial ruin.

1934–1938 Miller attends University of Michigan to study journalism, switches to English after receiving the university's Hopwood Award in Drama for *No Villain*; his plays address social issues, workers' rights and family conflicts, especially between fathers and sons.

1940 Marries Mary Slattery.

1944 *The Man Who Had All the Luck* premieres on Broadway but closes within the week, though receives Theatre Guild National Award. Not produced in UK until 1960.

1946 Miller encounters his Uncle Manny at a Boston regional production of *All My Sons*; he becomes part of the inspiration for Willy Loman.

1947 *All My Sons* premieres and wins several awards.

1948 Miller builds a 10 by 12 feet writing studio on land purchased in Connecticut and writes *Death of a Salesman* in six weeks.

1949 *Death of a Salesman* premieres and wins Pulitzer Prize. *New York Times* publishes 'Tragedy and the Common Man' (essay).

1951 Yiddish production translated as *Toyt fun a seylsman* by Joseph Buloff and Luba Kadison staged in Brooklyn, NY.

1953	*The Crucible* premieres.
1955	The one-act *A View from the Bridge* premieres alongside *A Memory of Two Mondays.*
1956	Divorces Mary Slattery. Subpoenaed to appear before House UnAmerican Activities Committee. Marries Marilyn Monroe. Revises *A View from the Bridge* into two acts to premiere in UK.
1961	Divorced by Marilyn Monroe.
1962	Marries Austrian-born Inge Morath, a professional photographer.
1964	*After the Fall* premieres and *Incident at Vichy* is produced later in the year.
1965	Miller is elected president of PEN International, an international literary organization.
1968	*The Price* premieres.
1974	Miller permits first production of *Salesman* within 100 miles of New York City in Philadelphia.
1978	Miller's first trip to China, with wife Inge Morath.
1979	Miller and Morath co-author *Chinese Encounters.*
1983	Miller directs Chinese production of *Death of a Salesman* at Beijing People's Art Theatre.
1984	Dustin Hoffman plays Willy Loman in *Death of a Salesman* at the Broadhurst Theatre.
1985	Made-for-television film of the above stage version.
1987	Miller's memoir *Timebends* is published.
1994	*Broken Glass* premieres.
1999	*Death of a Salesman* revived on Broadway with Brian Dennehy for the play's fiftieth anniversary.
2002	Death of Inge Morath.
2005	Miller dies of heart failure in his Connecticut home on 10 February.

Introduction

Historical, social and cultural contexts

In his autobiography, Arthur Miller stated, 'I could not imagine a theater worth my time that did not want to change the world.' With this lofty goal, as a college student, Miller embarked on his journey towards playwriting. Initially a journalism major, he shifted his efforts from trying to change the world through reporting the news to reflecting the impact of that news on theatre stages. Miller regarded theatre as the most direct form of communication with the public, and the form with the greatest transformative potential. His play *Death of a Salesman* fulfilled that potential. When it opened on Broadway in February 1949, reviews hailed it as 'one of the finest dramas in the whole range of American theater' and 'a play to make history'. It swept top theatre awards, was staged in every major American city within a year and was subsequently produced around the globe. Within a few decades it was already being called iconic, a classic, and hailed as a masterpiece; it retains those labels today, often ranked as the greatest American play of all time. Miller is considered an important public figure who spoke out on social causes in his plays, essays and public commentaries. When he died in 2005, the front-page headline called him the 'moral voice of the American stage'.

Socio-economic conditions

In April 2020, during the global COVID-19 pandemic, a journalist stated, 'America, reeling from the economic devastation of the Coronavirus crisis, is in the grip of a "Death of a Salesman" moment. As the pandemic lays waste to the economy, the play reminds us of the unchanging truth of an American dream dangled for the many but obtainable only by a ruthless few.' The *Los Angeles Times* article describes a scene from the play in which the main character Willy Loman approaches his boss Howard, and is turned away in spite of thirty-four years of loyalty. In response Willy defiantly utters one of the play's most famous lines: 'You can't eat the orange and throw the peel away – a man is not a piece of fruit.'

Circumstances in the early 2020s were not unlike the crisis that befell Miller's family in the 1930s during the Great Depression. When the stock market crashed, his father lost his business and also lost hope. After living as an upper-middle-class family in Manhattan overlooking picturesque Central Park, the Miller family moved to the working-class borough of Brooklyn, which would become the setting for the Loman family. The impact of this period of economic crisis on middle-class American families was all-encompassing: the financial strain took a psychological toll on marriages and fathers who could no longer provide for their families. The suicide rate reached an all-time high in 1933. *Salesman* is set in the wake of the Depression, when the economy was struggling to recover, and the nation had gone to war and back (the Second World War ended in 1945). Full recovery from the economic crash would take twenty-five years. Clearly, the Loman family had been impacted long before the action in the play begins: Willy's sales have been steadily declining, he is struggling to pay the mortgage, his car is not reliable, household appliances are in need of repair, and he is disillusioned, dishevelled and exhausted from the moment we first meet him.

Family structure and ethnic identity

Many of the characters, places and situations in *Salesman* are inspired by Miller's family and friends. As a teenager, he loved playing football, much like Biff, and was not much of a scholar. The Loman family is largely based on his uncle, Manny Newman, and his wife and sons. But the character of Willy went beyond Uncle Manny and included pieces of Miller himself – in 2000 he called Willy 'a segment of my flesh' and reflected that the character provided a 'vessel for many feelings [and] thoughts that had been floating in my head' ever since childhood.

The working-class milieu of 1940s Brooklyn in the play is the neighbourhood where the Millers lived. They were a Jewish immigrant family whose earliest roots in America were planted in the late nineteenth century fleeing Poland to escape the anti-Semitic violence of the Russian pogroms. Growing up in the Jewish enclave that Brooklyn was at the time, Miller was raised in a household surrounded by Jewish cultural traditions until he went to college, and would later self-identify as a secular Jew. The paradox in his own life of the rich impact of his Jewish identity pulsing below the surface of his direct interactions in the world is echoed in the way the Loman family in *Salesman* can be read as Jewish without being overtly identified as such. When this question arose after the play's premiere, Miller said there was nothing Jewish about the play, but decades later acknowledged that the Lomans are a Jewish family.

Genre and themes

Subjective realism

Salesman presented a new style of theatre to audiences in the United States and abroad. International theatre critics reviewing overseas performances described the play's departure from conventional realism with labels such as 'magic realism', 'neo-realism' and 'mythological realism'. All recognized its mixture of realism and expressionism. Expressionism, a form of art and literature that emerged in early twentieth-century Northern Europe, depicts the world not through a realistic lens attempting to imitate what is seen by the eye, but through a subjective lens that distorts colours and forms to represent moods, feelings and ideas. Having based some characters on people he knew, Miller gave specific descriptions of what they should look like, but he also said the play was conceived in two realms, with actual characters co-existing alongside others who function as symbols for Willy.

Initially choosing the title *The Inside of his Head*, Miller saw the set taking the form of a gigantic head with all the action occurring inside – a clear example of expressionism. But he dropped this idea in favour of the more realistic *Death of a Salesman*. The stage directions that precede Willy's entrance at the beginning of the play clearly express the dual reality he wanted to create both physically and psychologically, indicating that when moments in the play take place in the present, the boundaries of the 'walls' of the set are observed by actors, who only enter the house through the doorway, while during Willy's daydreams and memories set in the past, actors step 'through' the walls onto the forestage where those sequences occur. Miller regarded expressionism as a form for exploring social and moral forces, and realism as the form for dramatizing family dynamics, so he alternates and fuses these styles.

The American Dream

For many immigrants to the United States past and present, the American Dream has been the hope for individual freedom from political or economic oppression, war or other trauma – or the opportunity for a better education, or a better future for the next generation. For many Americans, the dream is equated with material gains like having a job, buying a home, and owning a car and other possessions, as well as perceived personal successes like getting an education, having a family and working hard enough to retire in good health. For others, as symbolized by Willy's brother Ben, the dream is to search for great adventures and wealth. All versions of the dream are rooted in independence and material comfort, and the belief that if one works hard enough, wealth and success are achievable. It is important to remember that the fruits of the American Dream are symbolic and access to the American Dream is not equal. The myth of the American Dream since the term was coined in the 1930s has been contradicted by immigration laws, systemic racism, anti-Semitism, inequality for women, homophobia and lack of mobility for the poor that continue to persist in the country.

For many in the 1930s–1940s, the American Dream seemed out of reach for these reasons and because of the social and economic impact of the Great Depression and the Second World War. These external factors are present in Willy Loman's story – the days of the travelling salesman are numbered and the different talents of a new generation are taking hold – but the poetic irony of Willy increasingly slipping into daydreams as his American Dream is slipping away indicates that internal factors are just as powerful. As a review of

Charles Dutton's performance in 2009 asserted, 'Willy's tragedy is not just one of society, but one of pride and arrogance of the individual.' Willy refuses to let go of the ideals he set for himself and his sons – ideals none of them have lived up to – and clings to illusions rather than facing the truth.

Fathers and sons

Miller acknowledged that his relationship with his father informed the play, but also that their real-life relationship was more like Bernard and Charley than Willy and Biff. It was his Uncle Manny, a travelling salesman who bragged about his two sons Buddy and Abby, who was more like Willy, while Miller's father was an ordinary businessman who didn't push his children. Though the title *Death of a Salesman* refers to Willy's demise, the play is as much about Biff as it is about Willy.

For both Willy and Biff, their own self-perception is inseparable from their expectation (even illusion) of the other. Biff recognizes this after the embarrassment of waiting for hours to seek a loan from Bill Oliver, who does not even remember him: 'I realized what a ridiculous lie my whole life has been! We've been talking in a dream for fifteen years.' He blames his father for his failure, saying that Willy's pumping him up is what led to his arrogance and difficulty working with others. In one of Willy's memory sequences we learn that Biff gave up on his own future and on Willy in high school when he went to Boston and discovered his father being unfaithful to his mother. Happy, meanwhile, is usually interpreted by critics as a younger version of Willy. He has lived in the shadow of his slightly older brother Biff, and has taken on his father's habits of exaggerating and lying. He openly boasts of his sexual conquests – even of fiancées of co-workers – echoing Willy's clandestine extramarital affair with The Woman in Boston.

The pairings of fathers and sons in the play (Willy and Biff, Willy and Happy, Charley and Bernard) also includes Willy and his own father, who is described in dream sequences, while his brother Ben and role model Dave Singleman (a legendary salesman) also function as father figures for Willy.

Gender and patriarchy

The world of *Salesman* is primarily a man's world. All of the major characters except Linda are men, while the only other female characters are The Woman, Jenny, Miss Forsythe and Letta. The latter three are minor, objectified roles of Charley's secretary and two prostitutes, and The Woman is a powerfully symbolic character (as is clear from her being unnamed) in Willy's past with whom he had an affair during sales trips to Boston.

Feminist critics such as Gayle Rubin have contended that women are constructed as objects of exchange and are denied agency in both the public and private spheres, and that this commodification of women is supported in part by the institution of heterosexual marriage. In this view, even Linda is relegated to the support role of wife and mother to the fully developed and complex male characters in the play. She functions primarily to care for and defend her husband, and he calls her his 'foundation and support'. At times, Willy directly exerts his power over her, even refusing to let her speak. This raises the question of how female images in *Salesman* might be received by today's audiences – are they outdated and potentially harmful representations, or can they be contextualized as Miller critiquing the patriarchal system of mid-twentieth-century America reflected in a play that renders women powerless?

In a 1985 interview, Miller said that female characters in his dramas have 'been played somewhat sentimentally, but that isn't the way they were intended'. While acknowledging that his female characters 'are of necessity auxiliaries to the action, which is carried by the male characters' he noted that 'they are forced to do that . . . the females are victims as well'. Specifically regarding Linda, Miller wrote that she is the kind of woman 'who is strong by concealing her strength' and that her part 'has often been weakly played, as though she were a mere follower, but that is unlikely to happen when the actress keeps herself aware of what the script has told her she knows'.

Mental health and suicide

Linda Loman is the only character in the play who knows Willy has attempted suicide and has left a rubber hose near the gas heater so that, in Miller's words, he might try again 'should the mood overtake him completely'. Miller emphasizes that Linda 'is fighting off his death from the outset'. Indeed, in her very first lines of the play, Linda asks Willy if something has happened, if he has crashed the car – foreshadowing the play's anticipated and tragic ending. 'Don't you feel well?' she asks as he enters, and he replies, 'I'm tired to death.'

Observing Willy struggle through his present, search his past for meaning and summon his dreams for a hopeful future, we become aware we are watching the demise of a man's spirit and, quite likely, the deterioration of his mind. Actors have played these aspects of Willy in various ways – from making him seem weak or depressed to defiant or even insane. And actors have always worn themselves out in the role, stepping into the body and mind of a man who enters the stage exhausted and exerts every ounce of energy he can muster as he progresses to his suicide by the end of the play. The mental and physical demands of the role have prompted formidable actors playing Willy to reduce the number of performances per week (Dustin Hoffman in 1984), leave the role months early (Lee J. Cobb and Paul Muni in 1949), or suffer psychologically as a consequence (Philip Seymour Hoffman in 2012). It is common for audiences to shed tears – something that Miller himself did not anticipate. He thought he had written a hard-hitting play and was at first disturbed that audiences were swept away by emotion, openly weeping and sniffling into handkerchiefs. But he said eventually he was pleased that the play impacted on people so profoundly, adding 'you can't make people see unless they feel'.

When *Salesman* was staged in Japan in 1984, an economic downturn had prompted a sharp increase in deaths by suicide among businessmen. Both suicide and madness are regarded differently in Japan and other areas in Asia than in the West, partly because of their frequent depiction in literary and theatrical traditions. For Japanese audiences, Willy descends into madness and that, combined with his loss of face (especially before his sons), leads to his suicide. Though Western critics avoid this interpretation, it is important to keep in mind that reception of plays by readers and audiences is culture-bound, and that the universality of characters and themes in *Salesman* leave them open to multiple readings.

Play as performance

The Role of Willy Loman

Miller imagined Willy Loman as a small man like his Uncle Manny, but performers of all types have been cast in the role. Opinions vary about the ideal age, size, appearance and personality of the actor. Miller tells us Willy 'is past sixty years of age' (life expectancy in the US was sixty-four years old in the late 1940s). In 1949 Lee J. Cobb was only thirty-seven, but in 2010 Christopher Lloyd played Willy at age seventy-two. Dustin Hoffman, small in stature like Miller had pictured, was forty-six when he played Willy. In stark contrast, it was a large looming Brian Dennehy in the role at sixty for the play's fiftieth anniversary revival. The magnitude, depth and demands of becoming Willy Loman are often compared to playing King Lear or other protagonists from Shakespeare's tragedies. Miller described Willy as 'a monster role, as exhausting as Hamlet, with so much of it demanding to be done at a high pitch. The play is without transitional scenes, when an actor can coast along for a while. Each scene begins at its latest possible moment, which means that Willy almost always enters in high gear.'

Language and translation

Death of a Salesman has been staged all over the world in English, but also translated into numerous languages including Chinese, Japanese, Korean, Hindi, Bengali, Tagalog, Spanish, Italian, French, German, Russian, Dutch, Danish, Swedish, Turkish and Yiddish. While contemporary productions in English face the challenge of how to make the Loman family drama of 1940s United States meaningful to twenty-first-century global audiences, productions in foreign languages confront additional questions of cultural transmission and linguistic translation. Young readers and audiences today experiencing the play in English may not be familiar with Ebbets Field, a Studebaker or 'chippies' – so imagine the challenge to a translator trying to convey these things, as well as transposing the lilt of Brooklyn cadence into an entirely different language, culture and time period.

In Yiddish, the Jewish identity of the Lomans came to the fore rather than being glossed over, and the audience experienced the play as if it had been written in Yiddish. According to one review in 1951, 'this production is really the original, and the Broadway production was merely Arthur Miller's translation into English'. Though visually imitating the original production and closely following Miller's script, names were changed (Biff and Happy became Bill and Harry), Yiddish idioms were added, Linda's character (played by Luba Kadison) became a strong Jewish mother and Joseph Buloff's Willy gesticulated with every line. Miller liked the production and gave Buloff and Kadison unlimited permission to perform the play in Yiddish, making this the only exception to his ban on all productions of *Salesman* within 100 miles of New York for 25 years.

A 2015 Yiddish production in New York City was performed on a mostly bare stage with English surtitles. Some scenes combined Yiddish and English, highlighting both the generation gap between Willy and his sons and the challenges (for the Lomans and the audience) of retaining Yiddish culture in the face of pressure to assimilate.

In China in 1983, Ying Ruocheng tackled the linguistic challenge by translating the dialogue into Chinese that incorporated local Beijing slang to create 'language that would have been spoken in a crowded Chinese city at the end of the 1940s'. When Daniel Yang directed the play in Taipei using Ying's Chinese translation, he replaced idiomatic Beijing expressions with Taiwanese.

One of Miller's strengths as a playwright is his adept handling of dialogue. The characters in *Salesman* and other plays come primarily from the working class and middle class, and their lines sound like things we recognize that common people would say, and yet they are not – Miller imbues the dialogue with a kind of eloquence that sounds common to us, but it has rhythm and poetry and slightly elevated language that sets it apart from everyday speech. A good example is Linda's reprimand of Biff when he comes home to visit and finds Willy disoriented. In response to Biff's disgust, Linda defends her husband, delivering a rhythmic speech of ten short lines that contains the most frequently quoted line of the play – 'attention must be paid' – followed a few lines later by another powerful (though deceptively simple) utterance: 'A small man can be just as exhausted as a great man.'

Setting the stage

Jo Mielziner's set design for the *Salesman* premiere in 1949 is one of the most iconic in American theatre, with rooms merely suggested by frames and a few set pieces – two beds, a refrigerator, a table and three chairs – cramped in a space between two building exteriors. With multiple levels and a neutral forestage space, the design created fluidity that allowed action to take place in both Willy's home and in his mind, and in both the present and the past. Many productions have retained these original design elements of set, lighting and music, while others have taken Mielziner's set design further towards minimalism or expressionism, as was the case with a Beijing Chinese production in 2012 and the Young Vic production in London in 2019.

Mielziner was also the show's lighting designer. His previous use of cinematic lighting effects combined with translucent scrims and combinations of realistic scenic elements with symbolic ones were just the right fit for the subjective realist style of Miller's play. Lighting is used to delineate scenes in real time from the flashback sequences, as well as to create the alternating environments of the present, when the Loman home is dwarfed by apartment buildings, and the past when there were two elm trees and plenty of sunlight. Each scene in the play flows into the next, with no changes of scenery or curtains or blackouts, creating a fluid unfolding of the story that matches the nimble meandering of Willy's mind and emotions.

Music is also important in the production, particularly Willy's 'theme' that is played on the flute during his entrance and throughout the play. The tune symbolizes Willy's absent father who was a travelling salesman peddling flutes.

Production history

Salesman has been produced all over the world by regional companies, community theatres, and on college campuses, including one of the earliest all-Asian American casts in an undergraduate production at Harvard University in 1997. The first professional production with an African American cast was in 1972 at Center Stage in Baltimore, Maryland, and the first Black man to play Willy in Britain was Trinidad-born Don Warrington in 2018 at the Royal Exchange, Manchester. Other Black actors, as well as East Asian, South Asian, Hispanic and Middle Eastern actors, have played the role of Willy in America and abroad, but most often the Loman family is cast as white. Wendell Pierce said that when he was cast for a British production in 2019, 'It was unexpected as an actor of color, I didn't expect to even have the opportunity.' He suggested that the universality of the play's themes is 'what makes it a classic . . . it speaks to humanity across time and place, age, race, gender. While it was written 70 years ago, it is relevant today, and it will be relevant 70 years from now.'

United States

After its Broadway debut in 1949 directed by Elia Kazan, with Lee J. Cobb playing Willy Loman, *Salesman* was revived on Broadway four times with four equally formidable actors taking on the iconic role: George C. Scott (1975), Dustin Hoffman (1984), Brian Dennehy (1999) and Philip Seymour Hoffman (2012). Dennehy was directed by Robert Falls in a production that premiered at the Goodman Theatre in Chicago in 1998 and moved to the Eugene O'Neill Theatre on Broadway in 1999 for the play's fiftieth anniversary. It featured a shifting modular scenic design by Mark Wendland – the Loman house separated and drifted apart into different configurations to underscore the action. Dennehy's performance as Willy was noted for the intensity that his large imposing frame and explosiveness brought to the role, contrasted with the tender sadness of the small man trapped inside. Elizabeth Franz's embodiment of Linda featured passion for Willy that, in Miller's assessment, was expressed as 'powerful protectiveness [and] fury' that had been 'washed out' in previous performances.

In 1974, George C. Scott had been granted permission to direct *Salesman* in Philadelphia – the first time Miller had allowed a production within 100 miles of Broadway – but Miller was so involved that he eventually stepped in to take over. A year later, Scott directed himself as Willy (in the round) at Circle in the Square Theatre in New York with Miller's blessing. Scott played Willy as tightly wound up and *New York Times* reviewer Clive Barnes exclaimed: 'There is nothing on earth like the magic of great acting . . . that leaves you in a state of grace, enables you to jump beyond yourself, to see something, that perhaps even the playwright himself only dimly perceived.'

United Kingdom

Barnes's highest praise, however, was reserved for the first British production of *Salesman*, directed by Elia Kazan six months after the Broadway production opened, using the same set and lighting design, costumes and music, and starring actor Paul Muni: 'I saw him six times and it was one of the acting performances I cherish in my heart.' Muni was born Frederich Meshilem Meier Weisenfreund in Galicia (now Ukraine) and his first language was Yiddish. He and his parents, both actors, emigrated to Chicago when he was seven years old and performed in the Yiddish theatre – Muni's first role in English was when he was thirty-one. As a stage and film actor, he was known for his extensive character preparation and transformation, but this resulted in Miller finding his performance as Willy to be too studied and technical.

Other notable productions in London were revivals at the National Theatre in 1979 and 1996, featuring Warren Mitchell and Alun Armstrong, respectively, as Willy Loman. In 2005, Brian Dennehy's Willy travelled to London in the first West End revival since Muni's performance – altogether, Dennehy took the stage more than 600 times. The second West End revival, directed for the Royal Shakespeare Company by Gregory Doran, opened in 2015 with Antony Sher in the role. This was followed by Marianne Elliott and Miranda Cromwell's direction of American actor Wendell Pierce as Willy in a British production that opened at the Young Vic in 2019 and then later in the year transferred to the Piccadilly Theatre, making it the third West End revival of the play.

Without any changes to Miller's script or any mention of race during the three-hour performance, the casting of the Loman family as African American in Elliott and Cromwell's production transformed the play and heightened its relevance, shining an unflattering light on racism as well as capitalism. Willy's struggle, while retaining its other psychological and social dimensions, also became the struggle of a black man trying to maintain his dignity and humanity in the face of racial inequality. As Sharon D. Clarke, who portrayed Linda Loman, explained, 'Willy breaks down because society was never going to allow him to achieve what he wants.' The stakes are heightened in terms of the danger Willy faces being out on the road: 'Think about Willy driving those 700 miles through states where he could be lynched simply for the colour of his skin . . . when he's in the hotel room with The Woman and he says, "I think there's a law about it in Massachusetts", that takes on a whole different connotation when you've got a black man and a white woman having a relationship in a time when there was segregation and there were lynchings.' Clarke added that Willy's white boss Howard calling him 'kid' becomes emasculating. Pierce, who played Willy, pointed out the increased tension when Happy as a young black man is asked if he'd rather sit in a different part of the restaurant. 'That kind of racial tension heightens all of Miller's words and makes you see them through fresh eyes', Clarke said. 'There are a whole slew of young people who will be seeing *Death of a Salesman* for the first time, and it will resonate so much more because it's a black family.'

China

The first Chinese production of *Death of a Salesman* (*Tuixiaoyuan zhisi* 推销员之死) was directed by Miller himself in 1983 at the Beijing People's Art Theatre, featuring Ying Ruocheng as Willy and Zhu Lin as Linda. Thirty years later the play was produced again at the same theatre in a very different version directed by Li Liuyi. In 1992 Hong Kong based director Daniel Yang (Yang Shipeng) staged *Salesman* in Taipei, Taiwan.

Ying translated the script and was Miller's creative partner in 1983. Together, they navigated the cross-cultural challenges of staging a major production during a period when China was still recovering from a decade of isolation and chaos during the Cultural

Revolution of 1966–76. It was unclear whether Beijing audiences in a communist society could sympathize with a travelling salesman or an ambiguous protagonist so unlike the heroes in socialist realism, but audiences identified strongly with the family bonds in the play, especially fathers and sons.

Miller kept a diary that later became his book *'Salesman' in Beijing*. One incident he describes is his struggle to convince the staff at the theatre not to use foreigner make-up and wigs on the actors, the common practice for roles in Western plays at the time. Without them, Miller believed the actors became 'Lomans-as-Chinese-looking-people . . . in some country of the mind . . . not in any earthly geography.' After he left China there were fifty performances in Beijing and a tour to Hong Kong and Singapore.

Li's 2012 version localized the story and evoked a trendy current-day Chinese vibe rather than a 1940s foreign feel. As both director and set designer, Li used only a few chairs, a table, a bench, a cluster of tree branches, the iconic refrigerator and numerous white spheres of varying sizes scattered across the enormous stage. Lighting effects cast looming shadows to create an expressionist feel, not unlike the scenography for the 2019 British production featuring Wendell Pierce discussed earlier.

In the 2010s–2020s in New York City and Vancouver, Canada, two separate projects were developed by two different playwright-director teams to stage the story of Miller and Ying's collaboration and their landmark 1983 production in Beijing, dramatizing the behind-the-scenes events integrated with scenes from Miller's original play as performed by the Chinese actors in 1983. Jeremy Tiang and Michael Leibenluft's *Salesman 之死 (zhisi)* and *Salesman in China* by Leanna Brodie and Jovanni Sy reflect the continuing relevance of *Death of a Salesman* and its international constellations on global stages today.

Academic debate

Scholars have written about *Death of a Salesman* from a multitude of perspectives, including formalist, Marxist, economic, feminist and psychoanalytic. While Marxist interpretations of *Death of a Salesman* consider the play a critique of the materialist illusion at the heart of the American Dream (as Marxism is concerned with class struggle and the impact of capitalism on ordinary working people), psychoanalytic approaches may focus on Willy's inner psyche, his illusions and denial, his crisis of conscience and ego, or his psychological breakdown. Depending on one's perspective, Willy has been interpreted as a failure, a fool, a victim or a fallen tragic hero. Miller describes his protagonist as a 'naked individual confronting the precepts of society' and Scottish actor Billy Mack who played the role in 2017 sees Willy as 'the wee man . . . who's trying to make it for himself and for his family, and it's just not working out'. This trope of the 'little man' is one that became a touchstone for the play's reception in productions both domestically and overseas. Brenda Murphy describes, for instance, how Austrian audiences in 1950 had no point of reference for the travelling salesman, but immediately recognized Willy as the 'little man' petty bureaucrat.

Is Willy Loman a tragic hero?

It is hard to imagine the diminished, defeated, diminutive person Miller modelled after his puny uncle as a tragic hero, when that term is usually assigned to the great personages of ancient Greek myth like Oedipus or Electra. And yet, *Salesman* has been credited as having reinvented the tragic hero as the 'common man'. In Aristotle's definition of tragedy that goes back to 335 BC, there is action that is serious and of great magnitude, usually a calamity befalling a heroic individual for whom the stakes are high and the dreadful event is devastating – and as a result of observing this, the audience experiences 'pity and fear' (compassion and dread) that result in an emotional catharsis (cleansing of emotions). This emotional arc is indeed similar to what both the protagonist Willy and the audience experience as the doomed salesman in Miller's play meets his inevitable destruction, but there are notable differences that have been debated since the outset. Atkinson was the first to call *Salesman* a 'tragedy' and said of its protagonist: 'Willy Loman is not a great man, but his tragedy is great.' But other theatre critics, such as John Gassner and John Mason Brown, disagreed, the latter opining that the play was a 'tragedy modern and personal, not classic and heroic', viewing Willy as a small man discovering his smallness, not a great classical hero destroyed by his greatness.

So heated was the debate that Miller responded with an essay published in *The New York Times* called 'Tragedy and the Common Man'. Without ever mentioning Willy Loman or the play, Miller asserted that any individual can experience and understand tragedy, not solely someone of substantial status or birthright: 'I believe that the common man is as apt a subject for tragedy in its highest sense as kings were.' While Miller uses 'man' and male pronouns in his essay, we should extend the argument to women and the common person in general. Citing Shakespeare's figures like Hamlet and Macbeth alongside their Greek counterparts, Miller maintains that tragedy occurs when someone is willing to lay down their life to preserve their personal dignity. The 'tragic flaw' that leads to the character's downfall in tragedy (often pride) is in Miller's formulation indignation and refusal to be passive. The quality in a play that rocks us to our core, he tells us, resonates in our own fear of displacement – of being ripped away from our self-image of who we are in the world – and that if we are destroyed, it is because of something wrong or dark in our environment, not ourselves. According to Miller, it is common people who know this terror best. He adds that although tragedy does not have to advocate revolution, 'no tragedy can come about when its author fears to question absolutely everything [and] regards any institution, habit, or custom as being everlasting, immutable, or inevitable'.

Are the Lomans Jewish?

Scholars have long debated the obscuring of the ethnic identities of the play's characters. Debra Caplan asserts their Jewishness was 'intentionally rendered invisible' in Miller's assimilationist masking of their ethnicity, while Henry Bial calls it an 'active disappearance' that results in dual codes that allow Jews to recognize the Jewishness of the characters while non-Jews do not. Earlier scholars used terms like 'crypto-Jewish characters' and 'ethnic anonymity' to describe the neutralizing or censoring out (as George Ross saw it) of the Loman's religious and ethnic identity. The first actor to play Willy Loman had himself changed his name from Leo Jacob to the ethnically neutral Lee J. Cobb, a common practice during and after the Second World War.

In bringing fully to light the history and content of the Yiddish production of *Salesman* that followed on the heels of the original play's premiere, Caplan makes a strong case for the importance of the Yiddish language in Jewish communities at the time, and the significance of 'counter-adaptation' (when a prominent cultural or literary piece in a dominant language is translated/adapted into a marginalized linguistic cultural or literary form and language with subversive and powerful results). Caplan reminds us that Miller 'refused to admit the Lomans were Jewish' until the fiftieth anniversary of *Salesman* at the turn of the twenty-first century, when he wrote in the preface that the Lomans were 'Jews light years away from religion or a community that might have fostered Jewish identity'. But she contends that to Yiddish audiences, Willy and his family have always been Jewish.

Behind the scenes – Chinese actor/translator Ying Ruocheng on working with Miller in Beijing

Ying's reminiscences of working with Miller in 1983 are also in his autobiography *Voices Carry: Behind Bars and Backstage during China's Revolution and Reform* (Rowman & Littlefield 2009). Excerpted from an interview conducted in 2002.

Impressions upon first reading *Salesman* in English in 1949

During my senior year at Tsinghua University, the librarian pulled me aside. She knew I was very keen on having a first look at the new books. The playwright had a name I didn't recognize – Arthur Miller – and the play was one I had never heard of – *Death of a Salesman*. So I took it away, and started reading it, and I finished it that same night. I was so drawn to the play, but immediately thought it would be impossible to produce at that time in China. It was only a couple months after the inauguration of the People's Republic, and [not] an appropriate time to introduce something like that. But it left a very deep impression on me. I was the president of the student drama club [and] I dreamed of staging *Death of a Salesman*.

Decision to stage *Salesman* in 1983

When Arthur and I were choosing a play to produce in Beijing in 1983, he suggested *The Crucible* because he had heard so much about persecution during his visit in 1978 – laments of intellectuals who were wrongly accused during the Cultural Revolution and so forth. I had to convince him to choose another play. I still had my eyes on *Death of a Salesman*, which had impacted me so strongly in my youth, and I wouldn't allow my unfulfilled dream of staging [it] to be shattered. So I tried my best to convince Arthur that just a story of persecution like *The Crucible* wasn't enough anymore. There would not have been any particular danger in producing *The Crucible* in the early 1980s, contrary to Miller's perception. In that respect *The Crucible* would not have been something new – whereas *Death of a Salesman* was truly a breath of fresh air, especially because of the way it was staged. For instance, the walls didn't exist for the people in the play anymore, especially for Willy Loman. He could walk through any wall and could communicate with whomever he was in the mood to. And Arthur created the necessary ambience for such things to be believable, to be credible. People were shocked – especially Chinese audiences, who were not accustomed to this kind of surrealistic style.

Task of translating *Salesman*

The original language of the play is very colloquial English, [so] my translation is heavily salted with Beijing dialect and slang. One has to take a middle way in translating a play like *Death of a Salesman* – the translator can't be completely faithful, but I don't think one should go too far into adaptation. For instance, the translator should not remove references to place names like Brooklyn and Yonkers – and, on the other hand, there is no need for actors to put on false noses and blonde wigs. The best result is when the play is performed and after five minutes the audience forgets about the actors' appearance and ethnicity, and buys into the belief that they're watching Americans – even if the characters don't look American. For our production, Arthur's verdict was that the Lomans were a second-generation Chinese family in Brooklyn. One day he said to the cast, 'You've done what I wanted. You look like a family, but a

Chinese family in Brooklyn,' which we thought was a funny way of putting it at the time. In 1983, none of us knew any Chinese families in Brooklyn, but we supposed it could happen.

Collaborating with Miller in rehearsals

Frankly, some playwrights are good at writing plays but know nothing about directing. Arthur Miller was extremely competent at both. He was able to give us a much deeper understanding of the play and its characters. Once, when Zhu Lin (the actress playing Linda) and I were having trouble concerning the relationship between Willy and Linda, Arthur told us he thought of Linda as having run away from home to marry Willy over her parents' objections. The audience knows nothing of this, but it helped immeasurably in our interpretation. During discussions at rehearsals, he was able to tell us a lot of things that we certainly couldn't imagine for ourselves. We could not cut anything in the text, even though the play ran longer than any play our theatre had ever produced. Miller used a stopwatch during rehearsal, saying: 'Congratulations! To the minute, the play in Chinese is the same as the play in English.' He also had a rich sense of humor – the two of us loved being together, and it seemed there was no challenge we could not solve with a joke.

Playing Willy Loman

Willy was certainly a tragic figure. But I had this incredible experience regarding his final realization that he had found a way to leave something behind for his son, Biff, to build a career on. Willy never lost sight of that career, and he came up with a plan to commit suicide in order to get the life insurance money. I remember I was on the stage by then towards the end of the play, when Willy appears with his brother Ben's ghost, who is giving him advice. He is exchanging ideas with his dead brother, and the more he describes his plan the more excited he gets. He becomes increasingly convinced that he can achieve this – that, thanks to him, his son will soon be holding twenty thousand American dollars and will begin a new career.

While onstage playing the role of Willy at this moment, I could hear the audience sniffling. The happier I got, the stronger the sniffling of the audience became. So in this case, we – the actor and the audience – were playing against each other. I was trying to convince them: 'Don't you see what a bloody good idea this is?' But somehow they just didn't understand. In this instance, the future that Willy paints for his son becomes very real, very true to life, and the more Willy thinks about it, the happier he becomes. But the audience went the other way, totally the other way.

The Beijing audience's reaction on opening night

[*Authorities at the theatre worried that the audience would not have the patience to sit through the Requiem scene, now that the main character had died and his story was over, and because the public buses stopped running at 10 p.m. and audiences would fear being stranded at the theatre – cars and taxis were not common in 1983, only bicycles and public buses.*]

And here's what happened. When the time came – after the car crash, which the audience recognized by the sound of it – I told the actors not to hurry, but to make their way onto the stage to the designated place (which was indicated by the lighting as Willy's tomb), and act out the scene seriously. And that's what we did. Miraculously, it worked. Nobody left the theatre. Nobody was even showing any impatience. In fact quite a number of spectators – a large fraction of the people there – were blubbering into their hankies. In other words, the play was a total success. I was waiting in the wings, while the other actors came off the stage one by one after paying tribute to Willy Loman. As the curtain came down, there was absolute silence from the audience for what seemed to us like a long time. One of our actresses started sniffling, thinking that the show was a total failure. And then, all of a sudden, I don't know who started it, but it came like an avalanche: the applause came forth and it didn't end. Everyone was cheering. I was relieved and excited – all of that effort had not been in vain. Nobody in the audience was concerned about the last bus. Instead of running out of the theatre as some of my colleagues had predicted, the audience rushed forward to the edge of the stage, shouting and pointing. This was the first truly successful new play since the end of the Cultural Revolution. This was a success with a capital *S*. The applause was unlike anything I had ever experienced as an actor. It was like a tidal wave. For an actor, this is the moment one lives for.

In the audience were a number of Americans and most of them did not understand a word of Chinese, yet even they were moved. You could see the tears streaming down their faces. And I saw the future of mankind – that we can communicate – not only intellectually, but emotionally. What we proved was that as far apart geographically and historically and in so many other ways as are the Chinese and the Americans, we are one humanity. We laugh at the same jokes; we cry the same tears; and we all love Arthur Miller.

Further study

Brater, Enoch, ed. *Arthur Miller's Global Theater.* University of Michigan Press, 2007

While this collection of essays by various scholars does not especially focus on *Salesman*, it provides chapters about Miller's influence and productions of his plays in Israel, China, Italy, South Africa, Germany, Dominican Republic, Ireland, Japan, Spain, Argentina, Denmark and the UK.

Caplan, Debra. '"Attention Must be Paid": *Death of a Salesman*'s Counter-Adapted Yiddish Homecoming.' *Modern Drama*, 58:2 (Summer 2015): 194–217

Article about Yiddish-language productions of *Salesman* in 1949 and 1951, and the importance of including them in Miller scholarship. See also Caplan's review of the 2015 production by New Yiddish Rep in *geveb: A Journal of Yiddish Studies* (November 2015).

Marino, Stephen. *Arthur Miller: Death of a Salesman / The Crucible.* Bloomsbury, 2015

Thorough study of both plays. Marino discusses the perspectives of almost every critic and scholar that has written about the plays in English up until the book's publication. Organized in chapters chronologically (from 1940s to 2000s) and by topics including early reviews and criticism; society and tragedy; salesmanship, psychology, ethnicity; feminism and gender; critical trends; film and TV versions.

Marino, Stephen, ed. *The Salesman Has a Birthday: Essays Celebrating the Fiftieth Anniversary of Arthur Miller's 'Death of a Salesman'.* University Press of America, 2000

Collection of papers from a variety of perspectives about *Death of a Salesman* delivered at the fifth Arthur Miller Conference in 1999. Essays by leading Miller scholars such as Christopher Bigsby, Susan Abbotson, Brenda Murphy, Matthew Roudané and volume editor Marino, who is also editor of another excellent resource, *The Arthur Miller Journal*.

Miller, Arthur. '*Death of a Salesman*' *in Beijing*. Bloomsbury, 2015

New edition of 1984 *'Salesman' in Beijing* published during the centennial of Miller's birth in 2015. New introduction by Claire Conceison provides historical overview of Miller's influence in China, including productions of his plays. Remainder of the book is in the form of Miller's diary entries during his stay in Beijing from March to May 1983 while directing the first Chinese production of *Death of a Salesman* at the Beijing People's Art Theatre. Contains behind-the-scenes information and cultural insights, full account of Miller's partnership with actor and cultural diplomat Ying Ruocheng, and detailed record of a ground-breaking cross-cultural collaboration.

Murphy, Brenda. *Miller: Death of a Salesman*. Cambridge University Press, 1995

One-third of the book provides detailed performance reconstruction of the original 1949 Broadway production. Other sections cover English-language productions of *Salesman* in the US, UK, Ireland, South Africa and Australia, and stagings in other languages including German, French, Spanish, Italian, Russian, Korean, Japanese and Chinese. A production chronology from 1949 to 1992 is included before the endnotes and extensive bibliography.

Death of a Salesman

Certain Private Conversations in Two Acts and a Requiem

The Characters

Willy Loman	**Charley**
Linda	**Uncle Ben**
Biff	**Howard Wagner**
Happy	**Jenny**
Bernard	**Stanley**
The Woman	**Miss Forsythe**
Letta	

The action takes place in Willy Loman's house and yard and in various places he visits in the New York and Boston of today.

Act One

A melody is heard, played upon a flute. It is small and fine, telling of grass and trees and the horizon. The curtain rises.

Before us is the Salesman's house. We are aware of towering, angular shapes behind it, surrounding it on all sides. Only the blue light of the sky falls upon the house and forestage; the surrounding area shows an angry glow of orange. As more light appears, we see a solid vault of apartment houses around the small, fragile-seeming home. An air of the dream clings to the place, a dream rising out of reality. The kitchen at center seems actual enough, for there is a kitchen table with three chairs, and a refrigerator. But no other fixtures are seen. At the back of the kitchen there is a draped entrance, which leads to the living-room. To the right of the kitchen, on a level raised two feet, is a bedroom furnished only with a brass bedstead and a straight chair. On a shelf over the bed a silver athletic trophy stands. A window opens onto the apartment house at the side.

Behind the kitchen, on a level raised six and a half feet, is the boys' bedroom, at present barely visible. Two beds are dimly seen, and at the back of the room a dormer window. (This bedroom is above the unseen living-room.) At the left a stairway curves up to it from the kitchen.

The entire setting is wholly or, in some places, partially transparent. The roof-line of the house is one-dimensional; under and over it we see the apartment buildings. Before the house lies an apron, curving beyond the forestage into the orchestra. This forward area serves as the back yard as well as the locale of all **Willy***'s imaginings and of his city scenes. Whenever the action is in the present the actors observe the imaginary wall-lines, entering the house only through its door at the left. But in the scenes of the past these boundaries are broken, and characters enter or leave a room by stepping "through" a wall onto the forestage.*

From the right, **Willy Loman***, the Salesman, enters, carrying two large sample cases. The flute plays on. He hears but is not aware of it. He is past sixty years of age, dressed quietly. Even as he crosses* *the stage to the doorway of the house, his exhaustion is apparent. He unlocks the door, comes into the kitchen, and thankfully lets his burden down, feeling the soreness of his palms. A word-sigh escapes his lips—it might be "Oh, boy, oh, boy." He closes the door, then carries his cases out into the living-room, through the draped kitchen doorway.*

Linda, *his wife, has stirred in her bed at the right. She gets out and puts on a robe, listening. Most often jovial, she has developed an iron repression of her exceptions to* **Willy***'s behavior—she more than loves him, she admires him, as though his mercurial nature, his temper, his massive dreams and little cruelties served her only as sharp reminders of the turbulent longings within him, longings which she shares but lacks the temperament to utter and follow to their end.*

Linda (*hearing* **Willy** *outside the bedroom, calls with some trepidation*) Willy!

Willy It's all right. I came back.

Linda Why? What happened? (*Slight pause.*) Did something happen, Willy?

Willy No, nothing happened.

Linda You didn't smash the car, did you?

Willy (*with casual irritation*) I said nothing happened. Didn't you hear me?

Linda Don't you feel well?

Willy I'm tired to the death. (*The flute has faded away. He sits on the bed beside her, a little numb.*) I couldn't make it. I just couldn't make it, Linda.

Linda (*very carefully, delicately*) Where were you all day? You look terrible.

Willy I got as far as a little above Yonkers. I stopped for a cup of coffee. Maybe it was the coffee.

Linda What?

Willy (*after a pause*) I suddenly couldn't drive any more. The car kept going off onto the shoulder, y'know?

Linda (*helpfully*) Oh. Maybe it was the steering again. I don't think Angelo knows the Studebaker.

Willy No, it's me, it's me. Suddenly I realize I'm goin' sixty miles an hour and I don't remember the last five minutes. I'm—I can't seem to—keep my mind to it.

Linda Maybe it's your glasses. You never went for your new glasses.

Willy No, I see everything. I came back ten miles an hour. It took me nearly four hours from Yonkers.

Linda (*resigned*) Well, you'll just have to take a rest, Willy, you can't continue this way.

Willy I just got back from Florida.

Linda But you didn't rest your mind. Your mind is overactive, and the mind is what counts, dear.

Willy I'll start out in the morning. Maybe I'll feel better in the morning. (*She is taking off his shoes.*) These goddam arch supports are killing me.

Linda Take an aspirin. Should I get you an aspirin? It'll soothe you.

Willy (*with wonder*) I was driving along, you understand? And I was fine. I was even observing the scenery. You can imagine, me looking at scenery, on the road every week of my life. But it's so beautiful up there, Linda, the trees are so thick, and the sun is warm. I opened the windshield and just let the warm air bathe over me. And then all of a sudden I'm goin' off the road! I'm tellin' ya, I absolutely forgot I was driving. If I'd've gone the other way over the white line I might've killed somebody. So I went on again—and five minutes later I'm dreamin' again, and I nearly—(*He presses two fingers against his eyes.*) I have such thoughts, I have such strange thoughts.

Linda Willy, dear. Talk to them again. There's no reason why you can't work in New York.

Willy They don't need me in New York. I'm the New England man. I'm vital in New England.

Linda But you're sixty years old. They can't expect you to keep traveling every week.

Willy I'll have to send a wire to Portland. I'm supposed to see Brown and Morrison tomorrow morning at ten o'clock to show the line. Goddammit, I could sell them! (*He starts putting on his jacket.*)

Linda (*taking the jacket from him*) Why don't you go down to the place tomorrow and tell Howard you've simply got to work in New York? You're too accommodating, dear.

Willy If old man Wagner was alive I'd a been in charge of New York now! That man was a prince, he was a masterful man. But that boy of his, that Howard, he don't appreciate. When I went north the first time, the Wagner Company didn't know where New England was!

Linda Why don't you tell those things to Howard, dear?

Willy (*encouraged*) I will, I definitely will. Is there any cheese?

Linda I'll make you a sandwich.

Willy No, go to sleep. I'll take some milk. I'll be up right away. The boys in?

Linda They're sleeping. Happy took Biff on a date tonight.

Willy (*interested*) That so?

Linda It was so nice to see them shaving together, one behind the other, in the bathroom. And going out together. You notice? The whole house smells of shaving lotion.

Willy Figure it out. Work a lifetime to pay off a house. You finally own it, and there's nobody to live in it.

Linda Well, dear, life is a casting off. It's always that way.

Willy No, no, some people—some people accomplish something. Did Biff say anything after I went this morning?

Linda You shouldn't have criticized him, Willy, especially after he just got off the train. You mustn't lose your temper with him.

Willy When the hell did I lose my temper? I simply asked him if he was making any money. Is that a criticism?

Linda But, dear, how could he make any money?

Willy (*worried and angered*) There's such an undercurrent in him. He became a moody man. Did he apologize when I left this morning?

Linda He was crestfallen, Willy. You know how he admires you. I think if he finds himself, then you'll both be happier and not fight any more.

Willy How can he find himself on a farm? Is that a life? A farmhand? In the beginning, when he was young, I thought, well, a young man, it's good for him to tramp around, take a lot of different jobs. But it's more than ten years now and he has yet to make thirty-five dollars a week!

Linda He's finding himself, Willy.

Willy Not finding yourself at the age of thirty-four is a disgrace!

Linda Shh!

Willy The trouble is he's lazy, goddammit!

Linda Willy, please!

Willy Biff is a lazy bum!

Linda They're sleeping. Get something to eat. Go on down.

Willy Why did he come home? I would like to know what brought him home.

Linda I don't know. I think he's still lost, Willy. I think he's very lost.

Willy Biff Loman is lost. In the greatest country in the world a young man with such—personal attractiveness, gets lost. And such a hard worker. There's one thing about Biff—he's not lazy.

Linda Never.

Willy (*with pity and resolve*) I'll see him in the morning; I'll have a nice talk with him. I'll get him a job selling. He could be big in no time. My God! Remember how they used to follow him around in high school? When he smiled at one of them their faces lit up. When he walked down the street . . . (*He loses himself in reminiscences.*)

Linda (*trying to bring him out of it*) Willy, dear, I got a new kind of American-type cheese today. It's whipped.

Willy Why do you get American when I like Swiss?

Linda I just thought you'd like a change—

Willy I don't want a change! I want Swiss cheese. Why am I always being contradicted?

Linda (*with a covering laugh*) I thought it would be a surprise.

Willy Why don't you open a window in here, for God's sake?

Linda (*with infinite patience*) They're all open, dear.

Willy The way they boxed us in here. Bricks and windows, windows and bricks.

Linda We should've bought the land next door.

Willy The street is lined with cars. There's not a breath of fresh air in the neighborhood. The grass don't grow any more, you can't raise a carrot in the back yard. They should've had a law against apartment houses. Remember those two beautiful elm trees out there? When I and Biff hung the swing between them?

Linda Yeah, like being a million miles from the city.

Willy They should've arrested the builder for cutting those down. They massacred the neighborhood. (*Lost:*) More and more I think of those days, Linda. This time of year it was lilac and wisteria. And then the peonies would come out, and the daffodils. What fragrance in this room!

Linda Well, after all, people had to move somewhere.

Willy No, there's more people now.

Linda I don't think there's more people. I think—

Willy There's more people! That's what ruining this country! Population is getting out of control. The competition is maddening! Smell the stink from that apartment house! And another one on the other side . . . How can they whip cheese?

On **Willy**'*s last line,* **Biff** *and* **Happy** *raise themselves up in their beds, listening.*

Linda Go down, try it. And be quiet.

Willy (*turning to* **Linda**, *guiltily*) You're not worried about me, are you, sweetheart?

Biff What's the matter?

Happy Listen!

Linda You've got too much on the ball to worry about.

Willy You're my foundation and my support, Linda.

Linda Just try to relax, dear. You make mountains out of mole-hills.

Willy I won't fight with him any more. If he wants to go back to Texas, let him go.

Linda He'll find his way.

Willy Sure. Certain men just don't get started till later in life. Like Thomas Edison, I think. Or B. F. Goodrich. One of them was deaf. (*He starts for the bedroom doorway.*) I'll put my money on Biff.

Linda And Willy—if it's warm Sunday we'll drive in the country. And we'll open the windshield, and take lunch.

Willy No, the windshields don't open on the new cars.

Linda But you opened it today.

Willy Me? I didn't. (*He stops.*) Now isn't that peculiar! Isn't that a remarkable—(*He breaks off in amazement and fright as the flute is heard distantly.*)

Linda What, darling?

Willy That is the most remarkable thing.

Linda What, dear?

Willy I was thinking of the Chevvy. (*Slight pause.*) Nineteen twenty-eight . . . when I had that red Chevvy—(*Breaks off.*) That funny? I coulda sworn I was driving that Chevvy today.

Linda Well, that's nothing. Something must've reminded you.

Willy Remarkable. Ts. Remember those days? The way Biff used to simonize that car? The dealer refused to believe there was eighty thousand miles on it. (*He shakes his head.*) Heh! (*To* **Linda**:) Close your eyes, I'll be right up. (*He walks out of the bedroom.*)

Happy (*to* **Biff**) Jesus, maybe he smashed up the car again!

Linda (*calling after* **Willy**) Be careful on the stairs, dear! The cheese is on the middle shelf! (*She turns, goes over to the bed, takes his jacket, and goes out of the bedroom.*)

Light has risen on the boys' room. Unseen, **Willy** *is heard talking to himself, "Eighty thousand miles," and a little laugh.* **Biff** *gets out of bed, comes downstage a bit, and stands attentively.* **Biff** *is two years older than his brother* **Happy***, well built, but in these days bears a worn air and seems less self-assured. He has succeeded less, and his dreams are stronger and less acceptable than* **Happy***'s.* **Happy** *is tall, powerfully made. Sexuality is like a visible color on him, or a scent that many women have discovered. He, like his brother, is lost, but in a different way, for he has never allowed himself to turn his face toward defeat and is thus more confused and hard-skinned, although seemingly more content.*

Happy (*getting out of bed*) He's going to get his license taken away if he keeps that up. I'm getting nervous about him, y'know, Biff?

Biff His eyes are going.

Happy No, I've driven with him. He sees all right. He just doesn't keep his mind on it. I drove into the city with him last week. He stops at a green light and then it turns red and he goes. (*He laughs.*)

Biff Maybe he's color-blind.

Happy Pop? Why he's got the finest eye for color in the business. You know that.

Biff (*sitting down on his bed*) I'm going to sleep.

Happy You're not still sour on Dad, are you, Biff?

Biff He's all right, I guess.

Willy (*underneath them, in the living-room*) Yes, sir, eighty thousand miles—eighty-two thousand!

Biff You smoking?

Happy (*holding out a pack of cigarettes*) Want one?

Biff (*taking a cigarette*) I can never sleep when I smell it.

Willy What a simonizing job, heh!

Happy (*with deep sentiment*) Funny, Biff, y'know? Us sleeping in here again? The old beds. (*He pats his bed affectionately.*) All the talk that went across those two beds, huh? Our whole lives.

Biff Yeah. Lotta dreams and plans.

Happy (*with a deep and masculine laugh*) About five hundred women would like to know what was said in this room.

They share a soft laugh.

Biff Remember that big Betsy something—what the hell was her name—over on Bushwick Avenue?

Happy (*combing his hair*) With the collie dog!

Biff That's the one. I got you in there, remember?

Happy Yeah, that was my first time—I think. Boy, there was a pig! (*They laugh, almost crudely.*) You taught me everything I know about women. Don't forget that.

Biff I bet you forgot how bashful you used to be. Especially with girls.

Happy Oh, I still am, Biff.

Biff Oh, go on.

Happy I just control it, that's all. I think I got less bashful and you got more so. What happened, Biff? Where's the old humor, the old confidence? (*He shakes* **Biff***'s knee.* **Biff** *gets up and moves restlessly about the room.*) What's the matter?

Biff Why does Dad mock me all the time?

Happy He's not mocking you, he—

Biff Everything I say there's a twist of mockery on his face. I can't get near him.

Happy He just wants you to make good, that's all. I wanted to talk to you about Dad for a long time, Biff. Something's—happening to him. He—talks to himself.

Biff I noticed that this morning. But he always mumbled.

Happy But not so noticeable. It got so embarrassing I sent him to Florida. And you know something? Most of the time he's talking to you.

Biff What's he say about me?

Happy I can't make it out.

Biff What's he say about me?

Happy I think the fact that you're not settled, that you're still kind of up in the air . . .

Biff There's one or two other things depressing him, Happy.

Happy What do you mean?

Biff Never mind. Just don't lay it all to me.

Happy But I think if you just got started—I mean—is there any future for you out there?

Biff I tell ya, Hap, I don't know what the future is. I don't know—what I'm supposed to want.

Happy What do you mean?

Biff Well, I spent six or seven years after high school trying to work myself up. Shipping clerk, salesman, business of one kind or another. And it's a measly manner of existence. To get on that subway on the hot mornings in summer. To devote your whole life to keeping stock, or making phone calls, or selling or buying. To suffer fifty weeks of the year for the sake of a two-week vacation, when all you really desire is to be outdoors, with your shirt off. And always to have to get ahead of the next fella. And still—that's how you build a future.

Happy Well, you really enjoy it on a farm? Are you content out there?

Biff (*with rising agitation*) Hap, I've had twenty or thirty different kinds of jobs since I left home before the war, and it always turns out the same. I just realized it lately. In Nebraska when I herded cattle, and the Dakotas, and Arizona, and now in Texas. It's why I came home now, I guess, because I realized it. This farm I work on, it's spring there now, see? And they've got about fifteen new colts. There's nothing more inspiring or—beautiful than the sight of a mare and a new colt. And it's cool there now, see? Texas is cool now, and it's spring. And whenever spring comes to where I am, I suddenly get the feeling, my God, I'm not gettin' anywhere! What the hell am I doing, playing around with horses, twenty-eight dollars a week! I'm thirty-four years old, I oughta be makin' my future. That's when I come running home. And now, I get here, and I don't know what to do with myself. (*After a pause:*) I've always made a point of not wasting my life, and everytime I come back here I know that all I've done is to waste my life.

Happy You're a poet, you know that, Biff? You're a—you're an idealist!

Biff No, I'm mixed up very bad. Maybe I oughta get married. Maybe I oughta get stuck into something. Maybe that's my trouble. I'm like a boy. I'm not married, I'm not in business, I just—I'm like a boy. Are you content, Hap? You're a success, aren't you? Are you content?

Happy Hell, no!

Biff Why? You're making money, aren't you?

Happy (*moving about with energy, expressiveness*) All I can do now is wait for the merchandise manager to die. And suppose I get to be merchandise manager? He's a good friend of mine, and he just built a terrific estate on Long Island. And he lived there about two months and sold it, and now he's building another one. He can't enjoy it once it's finished. And I know that's just what I would do. I don't know what the hell I'm workin' for. Sometimes I sit in my apartment—all alone. And I think of the rent I'm paying. And it's crazy. But then, it's what I always wanted. My own apartment, a car, and plenty of women. And still, goddammit, I'm lonely.

Biff (*with enthusiasm*) Listen, why don't you come out West with me?

Happy You and I, heh?

Biff Sure, maybe we could buy a ranch. Raise cattle, use our muscles. Men built like we are should be working out in the open.

Happy (*avidly*) The Loman Brothers, heh?

Biff (*with vast affection*) Sure, we'd be known all over the counties!

Happy (*enthralled*) That's what I dream about, Biff. Sometimes I want to just rip my clothes off in the middle of the store and outbox that goddam merchandise manager. I mean I can outbox, outrun, and outlift anybody in that store, and I have to take orders from those common, petty sons-of-bitches till I can't stand it any more.

Biff I'm tellin' you, kid, if you were with me I'd be happy out there.

Happy (*enthused*) See, Biff, everybody around me is so false that I'm constantly lowering my ideals . . .

Biff Baby, together we'd stand up for one another, we'd have someone to trust.

Happy If I were around you—

Biff Hap, the trouble is we weren't brought up to grub for money. I don't know how to do it.

Happy Neither can I!

Biff Then let's go!

Happy The only thing is—what can you make out there?

Biff But look at your friend. Builds an estate and then hasn't the peace of mind to live in it.

Happy Yeah, but when he walks into the store the waves part in front of him. That's fifty-two thousand dollars a year coming through the revolving door, and I got more in my pinky finger than he's got in his head.

Biff Yeah, but you just said—

Happy I gotta show some of those pompous, self-important executives over there that Hap Loman can make the grade. I want to walk into the store the way he walks in. Then I'll go with you, Biff. We'll be together yet, I swear. But take those two we had tonight. Now weren't they gorgeous creatures?

Biff Yeah, yeah, most gorgeous I've had in years.

Happy I get that any time I want, Biff. Whenever I feel disgusted. The only trouble is, it gets like bowling or something. I just keep knockin' them over and it doesn't mean anything. You still run around a lot?

Biff Naa. I'd like to find a girl—steady, somebody with substance.

Happy That's what I long for.

Biff Go on! You'd never come home.

Happy I would! Somebody with character, with resistance! Like Mom, y'know? You're gonna call me a bastard when I tell you this. That girl Charlotte I was with tonight is engaged to be married in five weeks. (*He tries on his new hat.*)

Biff No kiddin'!

Happy Sure, the guy's in line for the vice-presidency of the store. I don't know what gets into me, maybe I just have an overdeveloped sense of competition or something, but I went and ruined her, and furthermore I can't get rid of her. And he's the third executive I've done that to. Isn't that a crummy characteristic? And to top it all, I go to their weddings! (*Indignantly, but laughing:*) Like I'm not supposed to take bribes. Manufacturers offer me a hundred-dollar bill now and then to throw an order their way. You know how honest I am, but it's like this girl, see. I hate myself for it. Because I don't want the girl, and, still, I take it and—I love it!

Biff Let's go to sleep.

Happy I guess we didn't settle anything, heh?

Biff I just got one idea that I think I'm going to try.

Happy What's that?

Biff Remember Bill Oliver?

Happy Sure, Oliver is very big now. You want to work for him again?

Biff No, but when I quit he said something to me. He put his arm on my shoulder, and he said, "Biff, if you ever need anything, come to me."

Happy I remember that. That sounds good.

Biff I think I'll go to see him. If I could get ten thousand or even seven or eight thousand dollars I could buy a beautiful ranch.

Happy I bet he'd back you. 'Cause he thought highly of you, Biff. I mean, they all do. You're well liked, Biff. That's why I say to come back here, and we both have the apartment. And I'm tellin' you, Biff, any babe you want . . .

Biff No, with a ranch I could do the work I like and still be something. I just wonder though. I wonder if Oliver still thinks I stole that carton of basketballs.

Happy Oh, he probably forgot that long ago. It's almost ten years. You're too sensitive. Anyway, he didn't really fire you.

Biff Well, I think he was going to. I think that's why I quit. I was never sure whether he knew or not. I know he thought the world of me, though. I was the only one he'd let lock up the place.

Willy (*below*) You gonna wash the engine, Biff?

Happy Shh!

Biff *looks at* **Happy**, *who is gazing down, listening.* **Willy** *is mumbling in the parlor.*

Happy You hear that?

They listen. **Willy** *laughs warmly.*

Biff (*growing angry*) Doesn't he know Mom can hear that?

Willy Don't get your sweater dirty, Biff!

A look of pain crosses **Biff***'s face.*

Happy Isn't that terrible? Don't leave again, will you? You'll find a job here. You gotta stick around. I don't know what to do about him, it's getting embarrassing.

Willy What a simonizing job!

Biff Mom's hearing that!

Willy No kiddin', Biff, you got a date? Wonderful!

Happy Go on to sleep. But talk to him in the morning, will you?

Biff (*reluctantly getting into bed*) With her in the house. Brother!

Happy (*getting into bed*) I wish you'd have a good talk with him.

The light on their room begins to fade.

Biff (*to himself in bed*) That selfish, stupid . . .

Happy Sh . . . Sleep, Biff.

Their light is out. Well before they have finished speaking, **Willy***'s form is dimly seen below in the darkened kitchen. He opens the refrigerator, searches in there, and takes out a bottle of milk. The apartment houses are fading out, and the entire house and surroundings become covered with leaves. Music insinuates itself as the leaves appear.*

Willy Just wanna be careful with those girls, Biff, that's all. Don't make any promises. No promises of any kind. Because a girl, y'know, they always believe what you tell 'em, and you're very young, Biff, you're too young to be talking seriously to girls.

Light rises on the kitchen. **Willy***, talking, shuts the refrigerator door and comes downstage to the kitchen table. He pours milk into a glass. He is totally immersed in himself, smiling faintly.*

Willy Too young entirely, Biff. You want to watch your schooling first. Then when you're all set, there'll be plenty of girls for a boy like you. (*He smiles broadly at a kitchen chair.*) That so? The girls pay for you? (*He laughs.*) Boy, you must really be makin' a hit.

Willy *is gradually addressing—physically—a point offstage, speaking through the wall of the kitchen, and his voice has been rising in volume to that of a normal conversation.*

Willy I been wondering why you polish the car so careful. Ha! Don't leave the hubcaps, boys. Get the chamois to the hubcaps. Happy, use newspaper on the windows, it's the easiest thing. Show him how to do it, Biff! You see, Happy? Pad it up, use it like a pad. That's it, that's it, good work. You're doin' all right, Hap. (*He pauses, then nods in approbation for a few seconds, then looks upward.*) Biff, first thing we gotta do when we get time is clip that big branch over the house. Afraid it's gonna fall in a storm and hit the roof. Tell you what. We get a rope and sling her around, and then we climb up there with a couple of saws and take her down. Soon as you finish the car, boys, I wanna see ya. I got a surprise for you, boys.

Biff (*offstage*) Whatta ya got, Dad?

Willy No, you finish first. Never leave a job till you're finished—remember that. (*Looking toward the "big trees":*) Biff, up in Albany I saw a beautiful hammock. I think I'll buy it next trip, and we'll hang it right between those two elms. Wouldn't that be something? Just swingin' there under those branches. Boy, that would be . . .

Young Biff *and* **Young Happy** *appear from the direction* **Willy** *was addressing.* **Happy** *carries rags and a pail of water.* **Biff**, *wearing a sweater with a block "S," carries a football.*

Biff (*pointing in the direction of the car offstage*) How's that, Pop, professional?

Willy Terrific. Terrific job, boys. Good work, Biff.

Happy Where's the surprise, Pop?

Willy In the back seat of the car.

Happy Boy! (*He runs off.*)

Biff What is it, Dad? Tell me, what'd you buy?

Willy (*laughing, cuffs him*) Never mind, something I want you to have.

Biff (*turns and starts off*) What is it, Hap?

Happy (*offstage*) It's a punching bag!

Biff Oh, Pop!

Willy It's got Gene Tunney's signature on it!

Happy *runs onstage with a punching bag.*

Biff Gee, how'd you know we wanted a punching bag?

Willy Well, it's the finest thing for the timing.

Happy (*lies down on his back and pedals with his feet*) I'm losing weight, you notice, Pop?

Willy (*to* **Happy**) Jumping rope is good too.

Biff Did you see the new football I got?

Willy (*examining the ball*) Where'd you get a new ball?

Biff The coach told me to practice my passing.

Willy That so? And he gave you the ball, heh?

Biff Well, I borrowed it from the locker room. (*He laughs confidentially.*)

Willy (*laughing with him at the theft*) I want you to return that.

Happy I told you he wouldn't like it!

Biff (*angrily*) Well, I'm bringing it back!

Willy (*stopping the incipient argument, to* **Happy**) Sure, he's gotta practice with a regulation ball, doesn't he? (*To* **Biff**.) Coach'll probably congratulate you on your initiative!

Biff Oh, he keeps congratulating my initiative all the time, Pop.

Willy That's because he likes you. If somebody else took that ball there'd be an uproar. So what's the report, boys, what's the report?

Biff Where'd you go this time, Dad? Gee we were lonesome for you.

Willy (*pleased, puts an arm around each boy and they come down to the apron*) Lonesome, heh?

Biff Missed you every minute.

Willy Don't say? Tell you a secret, boys. Don't breathe it to a soul. Someday I'll have my own business, and I'll never have to leave home any more.

Happy Like Uncle Charley, heh?

Willy Bigger than Uncle Charley! Because Charley is not—liked. He's liked, but he's not—well liked.

Biff Where'd you go this time, Dad?

Willy Well, I got on the road, and I went north to Providence. Met the Mayor.

Biff The Mayor of Providence!

Willy He was sitting in the hotel lobby.

Biff What'd he say?

Willy He said, "Morning!" And I said, "You got a fine city here, Mayor." And then he had coffee with me. And then I went to Waterbury. Waterbury is a fine city. Big clock city, the famous Waterbury clock. Sold a nice bill there. And then Boston—Boston is the cradle of the Revolution. A fine city. And a couple of other towns in Mass., and on to Portland and Bangor and straight home!

Biff Gee, I'd love to go with you sometime, Dad.

Willy Soon as summer comes.

Happy Promise?

Willy You and Hap and I, and I'll show you all the towns. America is full of beautiful towns and fine, upstanding people. And they know me, boys, they know me up and down New England. The finest people. And when I bring you fellas up, there'll be open sesame for all of us, 'cause one thing, boys: I have friends. I can park my car in any street in New England, and the cops protect it like their own. This summer, heh?

Biff and **Happy** (*together*) Yeah! You bet!

Willy We'll take our bathing suits.

Happy We'll carry your bags, Pop!

Willy Oh, won't that be something! Me comin' into the Boston stores with you boys carryin' my bags. What a sensation!

Biff *is prancing around, practicing passing the ball.*

Willy You nervous, Biff, about the game?

Biff Not if you're gonna be there.

Willy What do they say about you in school, now that they made you captain?

Happy There's a crowd of girls behind him everytime the classes change.

Biff (*taking* **Willy***'s hand*) This Saturday, Pop, this Saturday—just for you, I'm going to break through for a touchdown.

Happy You're supposed to pass.

Biff I'm takin' one play for Pop. You watch me, Pop, and when I take off my helmet, that means I'm breakin' out. Then you watch me crash through that line!

Willy (*kisses* **Biff**) Oh, wait'll I tell this in Boston!

Bernard *enters in knickers. He is younger than* **Biff***, earnest and loyal, a worried boy.*

Bernard Biff, where are you? You're supposed to study with me today.

Willy Hey, looka Bernard. What're you lookin' so anemic about, Bernard?

Bernard He's gotta study, Uncle Willy. He's got Regents next week.

Happy (*tauntingly, spinning* **Bernard** *around*) Let's box, Bernard!

Bernard Biff! (*He gets away from* **Happy**.) Listen, Biff, I heard Mr. Birnbaum say that if you don't start studyin' math he's gonna flunk you, and you won't graduate. I heard him!

Willy You better study with him, Biff. Go ahead now.

Bernard I heard him!

Biff Oh, Pop, you didn't see my sneakers! (*He holds up a foot for* **Willy** *to look at.*)

Willy Hey, that's a beautiful job of printing!

Bernard (*wiping his glasses*) Just because he printed University of Virginia on his sneakers doesn't mean they've got to graduate him, Uncle Willy!

Willy (*angrily*) What're you talking about? With scholarships to three universities they're gonna flunk him?

Bernard But I heard Mr. Birnbaum say—

Willy Don't be a pest, Bernard! (*To his boys:*) What an anemic!

Bernard Okay, I'm waiting for you in my house, Biff.

Bernard *goes off. The* **Lomans** *laugh.*

Willy Bernard is not well liked, is he?

Biff He's liked, but he's not well liked.

Happy That's right, Pop.

Willy That's just what I mean. Bernard can get the best marks in school, y'understand, but when he gets out in the business world, y'understand, you are going to be five times ahead of him. That's why I thank Almighty God you're both built like Adonises. Because the man who makes an appearance in the business world, the man who creates personal interest, is the man who gets ahead. Be liked and you will never want. You take me, for instance. I never have to wait in line to see a buyer. "Willy Loman is here!" That's all they have to know, and I go right through.

Biff Did you knock them dead, Pop?

Willy Knocked 'em cold in Providence, slaughtered 'em in Boston.

Happy (*on his back, pedaling again*) I'm losing weight, you notice, Pop?

Linda *enters, as of old, a ribbon in her hair, carrying a basket of washing.*

Linda (*with youthful energy*) Hello, dear!

Willy Sweetheart!

Linda How'd the Chevvy run?

Willy Chevrolet, Linda, is the greatest car ever built. (*To the boys:*) Since when do you let your mother carry wash up the stairs?

Biff Grab hold there, boy!

Happy Where to, Mom?

Linda Hang them up on the line. And you better go down to your friends, Biff. The cellar is full of boys. They don't know what to do with themselves.

Biff Ah, when Pop comes home they can wait!

Willy (*laughs appreciatively*) You better go down and tell them what to do, Biff.

Biff I think I'll have them sweep out the furnace room.

Willy Good work, Biff.

Biff (*goes through wall-line of kitchen to doorway at back and calls down*) Fellas! Everybody sweep out the furnace room! I'll be right down!

Voices All right! Okay, Biff.

Biff George and Sam and Frank, come out back! We're hangin' up the wash! Come on, Hap, on the double! (*He and* **Happy** *carry out the basket.*)

Linda The way they obey him!

Willy Well, that's training, the training. I'm tellin' you, I was sellin' thousands and thousands, but I had to come home.

Linda Oh, the whole block'll be at that game. Did you sell anything?

Willy I did five hundred gross in Providence and seven hundred gross in Boston.

Linda No! Wait a minute, I've got a pencil. (*She pulls pencil and paper out of her apron pocket.*) That makes your commission . . . Two hundred—my God! Two hundred and twelve dollars!

Willy Well, I didn't figure it yet, but . .

Linda How much did you do?

Willy Well, I—I did—about a hundred and eighty gross in Providence. Well, no—it came to—roughly two hundred gross on the whole trip.

Linda (*without hesitation*) Two hundred gross. That's . . . (*She figures.*)

Willy The trouble was that three of the stores were half closed for inventory in Boston. Otherwise I would a broke records.

Linda Well, it makes seventy dollars and some pennies. That's very good.

Willy What do we owe?

Linda Well, on the first there's sixteen dollars on the refrigerator—

Willy Why sixteen?

Linda Well, the fan belt broke, so it was a dollar eighty.

Willy But it's brand new.

Linda Well, the man said that's the way it is. Till they work themselves in, y'know.

They move through the wall-line into the kitchen.

Willy I hope we didn't get stuck on that machine.

Linda They got the biggest ads of any of them!

Willy I know, it's a fine machine. What else?

Linda Well, there's nine-sixty for the washing machine. And for the vacuum cleaner there's three and a half due on the fifteenth. Then the roof, you got twenty-one dollars remaining.

Willy It don't leak, does it?

Linda No, they did a wonderful job. Then you owe Frank for the carburetor.

Willy I'm not going to pay that man! That goddam Chevrolet, they ought to prohibit the manufacture of that car!

Linda Well, you owe him three and a half. And odds and ends, comes to around a hundred and twenty dollars by the fifteenth.

Willy A hundred and twenty dollars! My God, if business don't pick up I don't know what I'm gonna do!

Linda Well, next week you'll do better.

Willy Oh, I'll knock 'em dead next week. I'll go to Hartford. I'm very well liked in Hartford. You know, the trouble is, Linda, people don't seem to take to me.

They move onto the forestage.

Linda Oh, don't be foolish.

Willy I know it when I walk in. They seem to laugh at me.

Linda Why? Why would they laugh at you? Don't talk that way, Willy.

Willy *moves to the edge of the stage.* **Linda** *goes into the kitchen and starts to darn stockings.*

Willy I don't know the reason for it, but they just pass me by. I'm not noticed.

Linda But you're doing wonderful, dear. You're making seventy to a hundred dollars a week.

Willy But I gotta be at it ten, twelve hours a day. Other men—I don't know—they do it easier. I don't know why—I can't stop myself—I talk too much. A man oughta come in with a few words. One thing about Charley. He's a man of few words, and they respect him.

Linda You don't talk too much, you're just lively.

Willy (*smiling*) Well, I figure, what the hell, life is short, a couple of jokes. (*To himself:*) I joke too much! (*The smile goes.*)

Linda Why? You're—

Willy I'm fat. I'm very—foolish to look at, Linda. I didn't tell you, but Christmas time I happened to be calling on F. H. Stewarts, and a salesman I know, as I was going in to see the buyer I heard him say something about—walrus. And I—I cracked him right across the face. I won't take that. I simply will not take that. But they do laugh at me. I know that.

Linda Darling . . .

Willy I gotta overcome it. I know I gotta overcome it. I'm not dressing to advantage, maybe.

Linda Willy, darling, you're the handsomest man in the world—

Willy Oh, no, Linda.

Linda To me you are. (*Slight pause.*) The handsomest.

From the darkness is heard the laughter of a woman. **Willy** *doesn't turn to it, but it continues through* **Linda***'s lines.*

Linda And the boys, Willy. Few men are idolized by their children the way you are.

Music is heard as behind a scrim, to the left of the house, **The Woman**, *dimly seen, is dressing.*

Willy (*with great feeling*) You're the best there is, Linda, you're a pal, you know that? On the road—on the road I want to grab you sometimes and just kiss the life outa you.

The laughter is loud now, and he moves into a brightening area at the left, where **The Woman** *has come from behind the scrim and is standing, putting on her hat, looking into a "mirror" and laughing.*

Willy 'Cause I get so lonely—especially when business is bad and there's nobody to talk to. I get the feeling that I'll never sell anything again, that I won't make a living for you, or a business, a business for the boys. (*He talks through* **The Woman***'s subsiding* *laughter.* **The Woman** *primps at the "mirror."*) There's so much I want to make for—

The Woman Me? You didn't make me, Willy. I picked you.

Willy (*pleased*) You picked me?

The Woman (*who is quite proper-looking,* **Willy***'s age*) I did. I've been sitting at that desk watching all the salesmen go by, day in, day out. But you've got such a sense of humor, and we do have such a good time together, don't we?

Willy Sure, sure. (*He takes her in his arms.*) Why do you have to go now?

The Woman It's two o'clock . . .

Willy No, come on in! (*He pulls her.*)

The Woman . . . my sisters'll be scandalized. When'll you be back?

Willy Oh, two weeks about. Will you come up again?

The Woman Sure thing. You do make me laugh. It's good for me. (*She squeezes his arm, kisses him.*) And I think you're a wonderful man.

Willy You picked me, heh?

The Woman Sure. Because you're so sweet. And such a kidder.

Willy Well, I'll see you next time I'm in Boston.

The Woman I'll put you right through to the buyers.

Willy (*slapping her bottom*) Right. Well, bottoms up!

The Woman (*slaps him gently and laughs*) You just kill me, Willy. (*He suddenly grabs her and kisses her roughly.*) You kill me. And thanks for the stockings. I love a lot of stockings. Well, good night.

Willy Good night. And keep your pores open!

The Woman Oh, Willy!

The Woman *bursts out laughing, and* **Linda***'s laughter blends in.* **The Woman** *disappears into the dark. Now the area at the kitchen table brightens.* **Linda** *is sitting where she was at the kitchen table, but now is mending a pair of her silk stockings.*

Linda You are, Willy. The handsomest man. You've got no reason to feel that—

Willy (*coming out of* **The Woman***'s dimming area and going over to* **Linda**) I'll make it all up to you, Linda, I'll—

Linda There's nothing to make up, dear. You're doing fine, better than—

Willy (*noticing her mending*) What's that?

Linda Just mending my stockings. They're so expensive—

Willy (*angrily, taking them from her*) I won't have you mending stockings in this house! Now throw them out!

Linda *puts the stockings in her pocket.*

Bernard (*entering on the run*) Where is he? If he doesn't study!

Willy (*moving to the forestage, with great agitation*) You'll give him the answers!

Bernard I do, but I can't on a Regents! That's a state exam! They're liable to arrest me!

Willy Where is he? I'll whip him, I'll whip him!

Linda And he'd better give back that football, Willy, it's not nice.

Willy Biff! Where is he? Why is he taking everything?

Linda He's too rough with the girls, Willy. All the mothers are afraid of him!

Willy I'll whip him!

Bernard He's driving the car without a license!

The Woman*'s laugh is heard.*

Willy Shut up!

Linda All the mothers—

Willy Shut up!

Bernard (*backing quietly away and out*) Mr. Birnbaum says he's stuck up.

Willy Get outa here!

Bernard If he doesn't buckle down he'll flunk math! (*He goes off.*)

Linda He's right, Willy, you've gotta—

Willy (*exploding at her*) There's nothing the matter with him! You want him to be a worm like Bernard? He's got spirit, personality . . .

As he speaks, **Linda**, *almost in tears, exits into the living-room.* **Willy** *is alone in the ktichen, wilting and staring. The leaves are gone. It is night again, and the apartment houses look down from behind.*

Willy Loaded with it. Loaded! What is he stealing? He's giving it back, isn't he? Why is he stealing? What did I tell him? I never in my life told him anything but decent things.

Happy *in pajamas has come down the stairs;* **Willy** *suddenly becomes aware of* **Happy***'s presence.*

Happy Let's go now, come on.

Willy (*sitting down at the kitchen table*) Huh! Why did she have to wax the floors herself? Everytime she waxes the floors she keels over. She knows that!

Happy Shh! Take it easy. What brought you back tonight?

Willy I got an awful scare. Nearly hit a kid in Yonkers. God! Why didn't I go to Alaska with my brother Ben that time! Ben! That man was a genius, that man was success incarnate! What a mistake! He begged me to go.

Happy Well, there's no use in—

Willy You guys! There was a man started with the clothes on his back and ended up with diamond mines!

Happy Boy, someday I'd like to know how he did it.

Willy What's the mystery? The man knew what he wanted and went out and got it! Walked into a jungle, and comes out, the age of twenty-one, and he's rich! The world is an oyster, but you don't crack it open on a mattress!

Happy Pop, I told you I'm gonna retire you for life.

Willy You'll retire me for life on seventy goddam dollars a week? And your women and your car and your apartment, and you'll retire me for life! Christ's sake, I couldn't get past Yonkers today! Where are you guys, where are you? The woods are burning! I can't drive a car!

Charley *has appeared in the doorway. He is a large man, slow of speech, laconic, immovable. In all he says, despite what he says, there is pity, and, now, trepidation. He has a robe over pajamas, slippers on his feet. He enters the kitchen.*

Charley Everything all right?

Happy Yeah, Charley, everything's . . .

Willy What's the matter?

Charley I heard some noise. I thought something happened. Can't we do something about the walls? You sneeze in here, and in my house hats blow off.

Happy Let's go to bed, Dad. Come on.

Charley *signals to* **Happy** *to go.*

Willy You go ahead, I'm not tired at the moment.

Happy (*to* **Willy**) Take it easy, huh? (*He exits.*)

Willy What're you doin' up?

Charley (*sitting down at the kitchen table opposite* **Willy**) Couldn't sleep good. I had a heartburn.

Willy Well, you don't know how to eat.

Charley I eat with my mouth.

Willy No, you're ignorant. You gotta know about vitamins and things like that.

Charley Come on, let's shoot. Tire you out a little.

Willy (*hesitantly*) All right. You got cards?

Charley (*taking a deck from his pocket*) Yeah, I got them. Someplace. What is it with those vitamins?

Willy (*dealing*) They build up your bones. Chemistry.

Charley Yeah, but there's no bones in a heartburn.

Willy What are you talkin' about? Do you know the first thing about it?

Charley Don't get insulted.

Willy Don't talk about something you don't know anything about.

They are playing. Pause.

Charley What're you doin' home?

Willy A little trouble with the car.

Charley Oh. (*Pause.*) I'd like to take a trip to California.

Willy Don't say.

Charley You want a job?

Willy I got a job, I told you that. (*After a slight pause:*) What the hell are you offering me a job for?

Charley Don't get insulted.

Willy Don't insult me.

Charley I don't see no sense in it. You don't have to go on this way.

Willy I got a good job. (*Slight pause.*) What do you keep comin' in here for?

Charley You want me to go?

Willy (*after a pause, withering*) I can't understand it. He's going back to Texas again. What the hell is that?

Charley Let him go.

Willy I got nothin' to give him, Charley, I'm clean, I'm clean.

Charley He won't starve. None a them starve. Forget about him.

Willy Then what have I got to remember?

Charley You take it too hard. To hell with it. When a deposit bottle is broken you don't get your nickel back.

Willy That's easy enough for you to say.

Charley That ain't easy for me to say.

Willy Did you see the ceiling I put up in the living-room?

Charley Yeah, that's a piece of work. To put up a ceiling is a mystery to me. How do you do it?

Willy What's the difference?

Charley Well, talk about it.

Willy You gonna put up a ceiling?

Charley How could I put up a ceiling?

Willy Then what the hell are you bothering me for?

Charley You're insulted again.

Willy A man who can't handle tools is not a man. You're disgusting.

Charley Don't call me disgusting, Willy.

Uncle Ben, *carrying a valise and an umbrella, enters the forestage from around the right corner of the house. He is a stolid man, in* *his sixties, with a mustache and an authoritative air. He is utterly certain of his destiny, and there is an aura of far places about him. He enters exactly as* **Willy** *speaks.*

Willy I'm getting awfully tired, Ben.

Ben*'s music is heard.* **Ben** *looks around at everything.*

Charley Good, keep playing; you'll sleep better. Did you call me Ben?

Ben *looks at his watch.*

Willy That's funny. For a second there you reminded me of my brother Ben.

Ben I only have a few minutes. (*He strolls, inspecting the place.* **Willy** *and* **Charley** *continue playing.*)

Charley You never heard from him again, heh? Since that time?

Willy Didn't Linda tell you? Couple of weeks ago we got a letter from his wife in Africa. He died.

Charley That so.

Ben (*chuckling*) So this is Brooklyn, eh?

Charley Maybe you're in for some of his money.

Willy Naa, he had seven sons. There's just one opportunity I had with that man . . .

Ben I must make a train, William. There are several properties I'm looking at in Alaska.

Willy Sure, sure! If I'd gone with him to Alaska that time, everything would've been totally different.

Charley Go on, you'd froze to death up there.

Willy What're you talking about?

Ben Opportunity is tremendous in Alaska, William. Surprised you're not up there.

Willy Sure, tremendous.

Charley Heh?

Willy There was the only man I ever met who knew the answers.

Charley Who?

Ben How are you all?

Willy (*taking a pot, smiling*) Fine, fine.

Charley Pretty sharp tonight.

Ben Is Mother living with you?

Willy No, she died a long time ago.

Charley Who?

Ben That's too bad. Fine specimen of a lady, Mother.

Willy (*to* **Charley**) Heh?

Ben I'd hoped to see the old girl.

Charley Who died?

Ben Heard anything from Father, have you?

Willy (*unnerved*) What do you mean, who died?

Charley (*taking a pot*) What're you talkin' about?

Ben (*looking at his watch*) William, it's half-past eight!

Willy (*as though to dispel his confusion he angrily stops* **Charley***'s hand*) That's my build!

Charley I put the ace—

Willy If you don't know how to play the game I'm not gonna throw my money away on you!

Charley (*rising*) It was my ace, for God's sake!

Willy I'm through, I'm through!

Ben When did Mother die?

Willy Long ago. Since the beginning you never knew how to play cards.

Charley (*picks up the cards and goes to the door*) All right! Next time I'll bring a deck with five aces.

Willy I don't play that kind of game!

Charley (*turning to him*) You ought to be ashamed of yourself!

Willy Yeah?

Charley Yeah! (*He goes out.*)

Willy (*slamming the door after him*) Ignoramus!

Ben (*as* **Willy** *comes toward him through the wall-line of the kitchen*) So you're William.

Willy (*shaking* **Ben***'s hand*) Ben! I've been waiting for you so long! What's the answer? How did you do it?

Ben Oh, there's a story in that.

Linda *enters the forestage, as of old, carrying the wash basket.*

Linda Is this Ben?

Ben (*gallantly*) How do you do, my dear.

Linda Where've you been all these years? Willy's always wondered why you—

Willy (*pulling* **Ben** *away from her impatiently*) Where is Dad? Didn't you follow him? How did you get started?

Ben Well, I don't know how much you remember.

Willy Well, I was just a baby, of course, only three or four years old—

Ben Three years and eleven months.

Willy What a memory, Ben!

Ben I have many enterprises, William, and I have never kept books.

Willy I remember I was sitting under the wagon in—was it Nebraska?

Ben It was South Dakota, and I gave you a bunch of wild flowers.

Willy I remember you walking away down some open road.

Ben (*laughing*) I was going to find Father in Alaska.

Willy Where is he?

Ben At that age I had a very faulty view of geography, William. I discovered after a few days that I was heading due south, so instead of Alaska, I ended up in Africa.

Linda Africa!

Willy The Gold Coast!

Ben Principally diamond mines.

Linda Diamond mines!

Ben Yes, my dear. But I've only a few minutes—

Willy No! Boys! Boys! (**Young Biff** *and* **Happy** *appear.*) Listen to this. This is your Uncle Ben, a great man! Tell my boys, Ben!

Ben Why, boys, when I was seventeen I walked into the jungle, and when I was twenty-one I walked out. (*He laughs.*) And by God I was rich.

Willy (*to the boys*) You see what I been talking about? The greatest things can happen!

Ben (*glancing at his watch*) I have an appointment in Ketchikan Tuesday week.

Willy No, Ben! Please tell about Dad. I want my boys to hear. I want them to know the kind of stock they spring from. All I remember is a man with a big beard, and I was in Mamma's lap, sitting around a fire, and some kind of high music.

Ben His flute. He played the flute.

Willy Sure, the flute, that's right!

New music is heard, a high, rollicking tune.

Ben Father was a very great and a very wild-hearted man. We would start in Boston, and he'd toss the whole family into the wagon, and then he'd drive the team right across the country; through Ohio, and Indiana, Michigan, Illinois, and all the Western states. And we'd stop in the towns and sell the flutes that he'd made on the way. Great inventor, Father. With one gadget he made more in a week than a man like you could make in a lifetime.

Willy That's just the way I'm bringing them up, Ben—rugged, well liked, all-around.

Ben Yeah? (*To* **Biff**:) Hit that, boy—hard as you can. (*He pounds his stomach.*)

Biff Oh, no, sir!

Ben (*taking boxing stance*) Come on, get to me! (*He laughs.*)

Willy Go to it, Biff! Go ahead, show him!

Biff Okay! (*He cocks his fists and starts in.*)

Linda (*to* **Willy**) Why must he fight, dear?

Ben (*sparring with* **Biff**) Good boy! Good boy!

Willy How's that, Ben, heh?

Happy Give him the left, Biff!

Linda Why are you fighting?

Ben Good boy! (*Suddenly comes in, trips* **Biff**, *and stands over him, the point of his umbrella poised over* **Biff**'s *eye.*)

Linda Look out, Biff!

Biff Gee!

Ben (*patting* **Biff**'s *knee*) Never fight fair with a stranger, boy. You'll never get out of the jungle that way. (*Taking* **Linda's** *hand and bowing:*) It was an honor and a pleasure to meet you, Linda.

Linda (*withdrawing her hand coldly, frightened*) Have a nice—trip.

Ben (*to* **Willy**) And good luck with your—what do you do?

Willy Selling.

Ben Yes. Well . . . (*He raises his hand in farewell to all.*)

Willy No, Ben, I don't want you to think . . . (*He takes* **Ben's** *arm to show him.*) It's Brooklyn, I know, but we hunt too.

Ben Really, now.

Willy Oh, sure, there's snakes and rabbits and—that's why I moved out here. Why, Biff can fell any one of these trees in no time! Boys! Go right over to where they're building the apartment house and get some sand. We're gonna rebuild the entire front stoop right now! Watch this, Ben!

Biff Yes, sir! On the double, Hap!

Happy (*as he and* **Biff** *run off*) I lost weight, Pop, you notice?

Charley *enters in knickers, even before the boys are gone.*

Charley Listen, if they steal any more from that building the watchman'll put the cops on them!

Linda (*to* **Willy**) Don't let Biff . . .

Ben *laughs lustily.*

Willy You shoulda seen the lumber they brought home last week. At least a dozen six-by-tens worth all kinds a money.

Charley Listen, if that watchman—

Willy I gave them hell, understand. But I got a couple of fearless characters there.

Charley Willy, the jails are full of fearless characters.

Ben (*clapping* **Willy** *on the back, with a laugh at* **Charley**) And the stock exchange, friend!

Willy (*joining in* **Ben***'s laughter*) Where are the rest of your pants?

Charley My wife bought them.

Willy Now all you need is a golf club and you can go upstairs and go to sleep. (*To* **Ben***:*) Great athlete! Between him and his son Bernard they can't hammer a nail!

Bernard (*rushing in*) The watchman's chasing Biff!

Willy (*angrily*) Shut up! He's not stealing anything!

Linda (*alarmed, hurrying off left*) Where is he? Biff, dear! (*She exits.*)

Willy (*moving toward the left, away from* **Ben**) There's nothing wrong. What's the matter with you?

Ben Nervy boy. Good!

Willy (*laughing*) Oh, nerves of iron, that Biff!

Charley Don't know what it is. My New England man comes back and he's bleedin', they murdered him up there.

Willy It's contacts, Charley, I got important contacts!

Charley (*sarcastically*) Glad to hear it, Willy. Come in later, we'll shoot a little casino. I'll take some of your Portland money. (*He laughs at* **Willy** *and exits.*)

Willy (*turning to* **Ben**) Business is bad, it's murderous. But not for me, of course.

Ben I'll stop by on my way back to Africa.

Willy (*longingly*) Can't you stay a few days? You're just what I need, Ben, because I—I have a fine position here, but I—well, Dad left when I was such a baby and I never had a chance to talk to him and I still feel—kind of temporary about myself.

Ben I'll be late for my train.

They are at opposite ends of the stage.

Willy Ben, my boys—can't we talk? They'd go into the jaws of hell for me, see, but I—

Ben William, you're being first-rate with your boys. Outstanding, manly chaps!

Willy (*hanging on to his words*) Oh, Ben, that's good to hear! Because sometimes I'm afraid that I'm not teaching them the right kind of—Ben, how should I teach them?

Ben (*giving great weight to each word, and with a certain vicious audacity*) William, when I walked into the jungle, I was seventeen. When I walked out I was twenty-one. And, by God, I was rich! (*He goes off into darkness around the right corner of the house.*)

Willy . . . was rich! That's just the spirit I want to imbue them with! To walk into a jungle! I was right! I was right! I was right!

Ben *is gone, but* **Willy** *is still speaking to him as* **Linda**, *in nightgown and robe, enters the kitchen, glances around for* **Willy**, *then goes to the door of the house, looks out and sees him. Comes down to his left. He looks at her.*

Linda Willy, dear? Willy?

Willy I was right!

Linda Did you have some cheese? (*He can't answer.*) It's very late, darling. Come to bed, heh?

Willy (*looking straight up*) Gotta break your neck to see a star in this yard.

Linda You coming in?

Willy Whatever happened to that diamond watch fob? Remember? When Ben came from Africa that time? Didn't he give me a watch fob with a diamond in it?

Linda You pawned it, dear. Twelve, thirteen years ago. For Biff's radio correspondence course.

Willy Gee, that was a beautiful thing. I'll take a walk.

Linda But you're in your slippers.

Willy (*starting to go around the house at the left*) I was right! I was! (*Half to* **Linda**, *as he goes, shaking his head:*) What a man! There was a man worth talking to. I was right!

Linda (*calling after* **Willy**) But in your slippers, Willy!

Willy *is almost gone when* **Biff**, *in his pajamas, comes down the stairs and enters the kitchen.*

Biff What is he doing out there?

Linda Sh!

Biff God Almighty, Mom, how long has he been doing this?

Linda Don't, he'll hear you.

Biff What the hell is the matter with him?

Linda It'll pass by morning.

Biff Shouldn't we do anything?

Linda Oh, my dear, you should do a lot of things, but there's nothing to do, so go to sleep.

Happy *comes down the stair and sits on the steps.*

Happy I never heard him so loud, Mom.

Linda Well, come around more often; you'll hear him. (*She sits down at the table and mends the lining of* **Willy's** *jacket.*)

Biff Why didn't you ever write me about this, Mom?

Linda How would I write to you? For over three months you had no address.

Biff I was on the move. But you know I thought of you all the time. You know that, don't you, pal?

Linda I know, dear, I know. But he likes to have a letter. Just to know that there's still a possibility for better things.

Biff He's not like this all the time, is he?

Linda It's when you come home he's always the worst.

Biff When I come home?

Linda When you write you're coming, he's all smiles, and talks about the future, and—he's just wonderful. And then the closer you seem to come, the more shaky he gets, and then, by the time you get here, he's arguing, and he seems angry at you. I think it's just that maybe he can't bring himself to—to open up to you. Why are you so hateful to each other? Why is that?

Biff (*evasively*) I'm not hateful, Mom.

Linda But you no sooner come in the door than you're fighting!

Biff I don't know why. I mean to change. I'm tryin', Mom; you understand?

Linda Are you home to stay now?

Biff I don't know. I want to look around, see what's doin'.

Linda Biff, you can't look around all your life, can you?

Biff I just can't take hold, Mom. I can't take hold of some kind of a life.

Linda Biff, a man is not a bird, to come and go with the spring-time.

Biff Your hair . . . (*He touches her hair.*) Your hair got so gray.

Linda Oh, it's been gray since you were in high school. I just stopped dyeing it, that's all.

Biff Dye it again, will ya? I don't want my pal looking old. (*He smiles.*)

Linda You're such a boy! You think you can go away for a year and . . . You've got to get it into your head now that one day you'll knock on this door and there'll be strange people here—

Biff What are you talking about? You're not even sixty, Mom.

Linda But what about your father?

Biff (*lamely*) Well, I meant him too.

Happy He admires Pop.

Linda Biff, dear, if you don't have any feeling for him, then you can't have any feeling for me.

Biff Sure I can, Mom.

Linda No. You can't just come to see me, because I love him. (*With a threat, but only a threat, of tears:*) He's the dearest man in the world to me, and I won't have anyone making him feel unwanted and low and blue. You've got to make up your mind now, darling, there's no leeway any more. Either he's your father and you pay him that respect, or else you're not to come here. I know he's not easy to get along with—nobody knows that better than me—but . . .

Willy (*from the left, with a laugh*) Hey, hey, Biffo!

Biff (*starting to go out after* **Willy**) What the hell is the matter with him? (**Happy** *stops him.*)

Linda Don't—don't go near him!

Biff Stop making excuses for him! He always, always wiped the floor with you. Never had an ounce of respect for you.

Happy He's always had respect for—

Biff What the hell do you know about it?

Happy (*surlily*) Just don't call him crazy!

Biff He's got no character—Charley wouldn't do this. Not in his own house—spewing out that vomit from his mind.

Happy Charley never had to cope with what he's got to.

Biff People are worse off than Willy Loman. Believe me, I've seen them!

Linda Then make Charley your father, Biff. You can't do that, can you? I don't say he's a great man. Willy Loman never made a lot of money. His name was never in the paper. He's not the finest character that ever lived. But he's a human being, and a terrible thing is happening to him. So attention must be paid. He's not to be allowed to fall into his grave like an old dog. Attention, attention must be finally paid to such a person. You called him crazy—

Biff I didn't mean—

Linda No, a lot of people think he's lost his—balance. But you don't have to be very smart to know what his trouble is. The man is exhausted.

Happy Sure!

Linda A small man can be just as exhausted as a great man. He works for a company thirty-six years this March, opens up unheard of territories to their trademark, and now in his old age they take his salary away.

Happy (*indignantly*) I didn't know that, Mom.

Linda You never asked, my dear! Now that you get your spending money someplace else you don't trouble your mind with him.

Happy But I gave you money last—

Linda Christmas time, fifty dollars! To fix the hot water it cost ninety-seven fifty! For five weeks he's been on straight commission, like a beginner, an unknown!

Biff Those ungrateful bastards!

Linda Are they any worse than his sons? When he brought them business, when he was young, they were glad to see him. But now his old friends, the old buyers that loved him so and always found some order to hand him in a pinch—they're all dead, retired. He used to be able to make six, seven calls a day in Boston. Now he takes his valises out of the car and puts them back and takes them out again and he's exhausted. Instead of walking he talks now. He drives seven hundred miles, and when he gets there no one knows him any more, no one welcomes him. And what goes through a man's mind, driving seven hundred miles home without having earned a cent? Why shouldn't he talk to himself? Why? When he has to go to Charley and borrow fifty dollars a week and pretend to me that it's his pay? How long can that go on? How long? You see what I'm sitting here and waiting for? And you tell me he has no character? The man who never worked a day but for your benefit?

When does he get the medal for that? Is this his reward—to turn around at the age of sixty-three and find his sons, who he loved better than his life, one a philandering bum—

Happy Mom!

Linda That's all you are, my baby! (*To* **Biff**:) And you! What happened to the love you had for him? You were such pals! How you used to talk to him on the phone every night! How lonely he was till he could come home to you!

Biff All right, Mom. I'll live here in my room, and I'll get a job. I'll keep away from him, that's all.

Linda No, Biff. You can't stay here and fight all the time.

Biff He threw me out of this house, remember that.

Linda Why did he do that? I never knew why.

Biff Because I know he's a fake and he doesn't like anybody around who knows!

Linda Why a fake? In what way? What do you mean?

Biff Just don't lay it all at my feet. It's between me and him—that's all I have to say. I'll chip in from now on. He'll settle for half my pay check. He'll be all right. I'm going to bed. (*He starts for the stairs.*)

Linda He won't be all right.

Biff (*turning on the stairs, furiously*) I hate this city and I'll stay here. Now what do you want?

Linda He's dying, Biff.

Happy *turns quickly to her, shocked.*

Biff (*after a pause*) Why is he dying?

Linda He's been trying to kill himself.

Biff (*with great horror*) How?

Linda I live from day to day.

Biff What're you talking about?

Linda Remember I wrote you that he smashed up the car again? In February?

Biff Well?

Linda The insurance inspector came. He said that they have evidence. That all these accidents in the last year—weren't—weren't—accidents.

Happy How can they tell that? That's a lie.

Linda It seems there's a woman . . . (*She takes a breath as*)

Biff (*sharply but contained*)} What woman?

Linda (*simultaneously*)} . . . and this woman . . .

Linda What?

Biff Nothing. Go ahead.

Linda What did you say?

Biff Nothing. I just said, "What woman?"

Happy What about her?

Linda Well, it seems she was walking down the road and saw his car. She says that he wasn't driving fast at all, and that he didn't skid. She says he came to that little bridge, and then deliberately smashed into the railing, and it was only the shallowness of the water that saved him.

Biff Oh, no, he probably just fell asleep again.

Linda I don't think he fell asleep.

Biff Why not?

Linda Last month . . . (*With great difficulty:*) Oh, boys, it's so hard to say a thing like this! He's just a big stupid man to you, but I tell you there's more good in him than in many other people. (*She chokes, wipes her eyes.*) I was looking for a fuse. The lights blew out, and I went down the cellar. And behind the fuse box—it happened to fall out—was a length of rubber pipe—just short.

Happy No kidding?

Linda There's a little attachment on the end of it. I knew right away. And sure enough, on the bottom of the water heater there's a new little nipple on the gas pipe.

Happy (*angrily*) That—jerk.

Biff Did you have it taken off?

Linda I'm—I'm ashamed to. How can I mention it to him? Every day I go down and take away that little rubber pipe. But, when he comes home, I put it back where it was. How can I insult him that way? I don't know what to do. I live from day to day, boys. I tell you, I know every thought in his mind. It sounds so old-fashioned and silly, but I tell you he put his whole life into you and you've turned your backs on him. (*She is bent over in the chair, weeping, her face in her hands.*) Biff, I swear to God! Biff, his life is in your hands!

Happy (*to* **Biff**) How do you like that damned fool!

Biff (*kissing her*) All right, pal, all right. It's all settled now. I've been remiss. I know that, Mom. But now I'll stay, and I swear to you, I'll apply myself. (*Kneeling in front of her, in a fever of self-reproach:*) It's just—you see, Mom, I don't fit in business. Not that I won't try. I'll try, and I'll make good.

Happy Sure you will. The trouble with you in business was you never tried to please people.

Biff I know, I—

Happy Like when you worked for Harrison's. Bob Harrison said you were tops, and then you go and do some damn fool thing like whistling whole songs in the elevator like a comedian.

Biff (*against* **Happy**) So what? I like to whistle sometimes.

Happy You don't raise a guy to a responsible job who whistles in the elevator!

Linda Well, don't argue about it now.

Happy Like when you'd go off and swim in the middle of the day instead of taking the line around.

Biff (*his resentment rising*) Well, don't you run off? You take off sometimes, don't you? On a nice summer day?

Happy Yeah, but I cover myself!

Linda Boys!

Happy If I'm going to take a fade the boss can call any number where I'm supposed to be and they'll swear to him that I just left. I'll tell you something that I hate to say, Biff, but in the business world some of them think you're crazy.

Biff (*angered*) Screw the business world!

Happy All right, screw it! Great, but cover yourself!

Linda Hap, Hap!

Biff I don't care what they think! They've laughed at Dad for years, and you know why? Because we don't belong in this nut-house of a city! We should be mixing cement on some open plain, or—or carpenters. A carpenter is allowed to whistle!

Willy *walks in from the entrance of the house, at left.*

Willy Even your grandfather was better than a carpenter. (*Pause. They watch him.*) You never grew up. Bernard does not whistle in the elevator, I assure you.

Biff (*as though to laugh* **Willy** *out of it*) Yeah, but you do, Pop.

Willy I never in my life whistled in an elevator! And who in the business world thinks I'm crazy?

Biff I didn't mean it like that, Pop. Now don't make a whole thing out of it, will ya?

Willy Go back to the West! Be a carpenter, a cowboy, enjoy yourself!

Linda Willy, he was just saying—

Willy I heard what he said!

Happy (*trying to quiet* **Willy**) Hey, Pop, come on now . . .

Willy (*continuing over* **Happy***'s line*) They laugh at me, heh? Go to Filene's, go to the Hub, go to Slattery's, Boston. Call out the name Willy Loman and see what happens! Big shot!

Biff All right, Pop.

Willy Big!

Biff All right!

Willy Why do you always insult me?

Biff I didn't say a word. (*To* **Linda***:*) Did I say a word?

Linda He didn't say anything, Willy.

Willy (*going to the doorway of the living-room*) All right, good night, good night.

Linda Willy, dear, he just decided . . .

Willy (*to* **Biff**) If you get tired hanging around tomorrow, paint the ceiling I put up in the living-room.

Biff I'm leaving early tomorrow.

Happy He's going to see Bill Oliver, Pop.

Willy (*interestedly*) Oliver? For what?

Biff (*with reserve, but trying, trying*) He always said he'd stake me. I'd like to go into business, so maybe I can take him up on it.

Linda Isn't that wonderful?

Willy Don't interrupt. What's wonderful about it? There's fifty men in the City of New York who'd stake him. (*To* **Biff***:*) Sporting goods?

Biff I guess so. I know something about it and—

Willy He knows something about it! You know sporting goods better than Spalding, for God's sake! How much is he giving you?

Biff I don't know, I didn't even see him yet, but—

Willy Then what're you talkin' about?

Biff (*getting angry*) Well, all I said was I'm gonna see him, that's all!

Willy (*turning away*) Ah, you're counting your chickens again.

Biff (*starting left for the stairs*) Oh, Jesus, I'm going to sleep!

Willy (*calling after him*) Don't curse in this house!

Biff (*turning*) Since when did you get so clean?

Happy (*trying to stop them*) Wait a . . .

Willy Don't use that language to me! I won't have it!

Happy (*grabbing* **Biff**, *shouts*) Wait a minute! I got an idea. I got a feasible idea. Come here, Biff, let's talk this over now, let's talk some sense here. When I was down in Florida last time, I thought of a great idea to sell sporting goods. It just came back to me. You and I, Biff—we have a line, the Loman Line. We train a couple of weeks, and put on a couple of exhibitions, see?

Willy That's an idea!

Happy Wait! We form two basketball teams, see? Two waterpolo teams. We play each other. It's a million dollars' worth of publicity. Two brothers, see? The Loman Brothers. Displays in the Royal Palms—all the hotels. And banners over the ring and the basketball court: "Loman Brothers." Baby, we could sell sporting goods!

Willy That is a one-million-dollar idea!

Linda Marvelous!

Biff I'm in great shape as far as that's concerned.

Happy And the beauty of it is, Biff, it wouldn't be like a business. We'd be out playin' ball again . . .

Biff (*enthused*) Yeah, that's . . .

Willy Million-dollar . . .

Happy And you wouldn't get fed up with it, Biff. It'd be the family again. There'd be the old honor, and comradeship, and if you wanted to go off for a swim or somethin'—well, you'd do it! Without some smart cooky gettin' up ahead of you!

Willy Lick the world! You guys together could absolutely lick the civilized world.

Biff I'll see Oliver tomorrow. Hap, if we could work that out . . .

Linda Maybe things are beginning to—

Willy (*wildly enthused, to* **Linda**) Stop interrupting! (*To* **Biff**:) But don't wear sport jacket and slacks when you see Oliver.

Biff No, I'll—

Willy A business suit, and talk as little as possible, and don't crack any jokes.

Biff He did like me. Always liked me.

Linda He loved you!

Willy (*to* **Linda**) Will you stop! (*To* **Biff**:) Walk in very serious. You are not applying for a boy's job. Money is to pass. Be quiet, fine, and serious. Everybody likes a kidder, but nobody lends him money.

Happy I'll try to get some myself, Biff. I'm sure I can.

Willy I see great things for you kids, I think your troubles are over. But remember, start big and you'll end big. Ask for fifteen. How much you gonna ask for?

Biff Gee, I don't know—

Willy And don't say "Gee." "Gee" is a boy's word. A man walking in for fifteen thousand dollars does not say "Gee!"

Biff Ten, I think, would be top though.

Willy Don't be so modest. You always started too low. Walk in with a big laugh. Don't look worried. Start off with a couple of your good stories to lighten things up. It's not what you say, it's how you say it—because personality always wins the day.

Linda Oliver always thought the highest of him—

Willy Will you let me talk?

Biff Don't yell at her, Pop, will ya?

Willy (*angrily*) I was talking, wasn't I?

Biff I don't like you yelling at her all the time, and I'm tellin' you, that's all.

Willy What're you, takin' over this house?

Linda Willy—

Willy (*turning on her*) Don't take his side all the time, goddammit!

Biff (*furiously*) Stop yelling at her!

Willy (*suddenly pulling on his cheek, beaten down, guilt ridden*) Give my best to Bill Oliver—he may remember me. (*He exits through the living-room doorway.*)

Linda (*her voice subdued*) What'd you have to start that for? (**Biff** *turns away.*) You see how sweet he was as soon as you talked hopefully? (*She goes over to* **Biff**.) Come up and say good night to him. Don't let him go to bed that way.

Happy Come on, Biff, let's buck him up.

Linda Please, dear. Just say good night. It takes so little to make him happy. Come. (*She goes through the living-room doorway, calling upstairs from within the living-room:*) Your pajamas are hanging in the bathroom, Willy!

Happy (*looking toward where* **Linda** *went out*) What a woman! They broke the mold when they made her. You know that, Biff?

Biff He's off salary. My God, working on commission!

Happy Well, let's face it: he's no hot-shot selling man. Except that sometimes, you have to admit, he's a sweet personality.

Biff (*deciding*) Lend me ten bucks, will ya? I want to buy some new ties.

Happy I'll take you to a place I know. Beautiful stuff. Wear one of my striped shirts tomorrow.

Biff She got gray. Mom got awful old. Gee, I'm gonna go in to Oliver tomorrow and knock him for a—

Happy Come on up. Tell that to Dad. Let's give him a whirl. Come on.

Biff (*steamed up*) You know, with ten thousand bucks, boy!

Happy (*as they go into the living-room*) That's the talk, Biff, that's the first time I've heard the old confidence out of you! (*From within the living-room, fading off:*) You're gonna live with me, kid, and any babe you want just say the word . . . (*The last lines are hardly heard. They are mounting the stairs to their parents' bedroom.*)

Linda (*entering her bedroom and addressing* **Willy**, *who is in the bathroom. She is straightening the bed for him*) Can you do anything about the shower? It drips.

Willy (*from the bathroom*) All of a sudden everything falls to pieces! Goddam plumbing, oughta be sued, those people. I hardly finished putting it in and the thing . . . (*His words rumble off.*)

Linda I'm just wondering if Oliver will remember him. You think he might?

Willy (*coming out of the bathroom in his pajamas*) Remember him? What's the matter with you, you crazy? If he'd've stayed with Oliver he'd be on top by now! Wait'll Oliver gets a look at him. You don't know the average caliber any more. The average young man today (*he is getting into bed*) is got a caliber of zero. Greatest thing in the world for him was to bum around.

Biff *and* **Happy** *enter the bedroom. Slight pause.*

Willy (*stops short, looking at* **Biff**) Glad to hear it, boy.

Happy He wanted to say good night to you, sport.

Willy (*to* **Biff**) Yeah. Knock him dead, boy. What'd you want to tell me?

Biff Just take it easy, Pop. Good night. (*He turns to go.*)

Willy (*unable to resist*) And if anything falls off the desk while you're talking to him—like a package or something—don't you pick it up. They have office boys for that.

Linda I'll make a big breakfast—

Willy Will you let me finish? (*To* **Biff**:) Tell him you were in the business in the West. Not farm work.

Biff All right, Dad.

Linda I think everything—

Willy (*going right through her speech*) And don't undersell yourself. No less than fifteen thousand dollars.

Biff (*unable to bear him*) Okay. Good night, Mom. (*He starts moving.*)

Willy Because you got a greatness in you, Biff, remember that. You got all kinds a greatness . . . (*He lies back, exhausted.* **Biff** *walks out.*)

Linda (*calling after* **Biff**) Sleep well, darling!

Happy I'm gonna get married, Mom. I wanted to tell you.

Linda Go to sleep, dear.

Happy (*going*) I just wanted to tell you.

Willy Keep up the good work. (**Happy** *exits.*) God . . . remember that Ebbets Field game? The championship of the city?

Linda Just rest. Should I sing to you?

Willy Yeah. Sing to me. (**Linda** *hums a soft lullaby.*) When that team came out—he was the tallest, remember?

Linda Oh, yes. And in gold.

Biff *enters the darkened kitchen, takes a cigarette, and leaves the house. He comes downstage into a golden pool of light. He smokes, staring at the night.*

Willy Like a young god. Hercules—something like that. And the sun, the sun all around him. Remember how he waved to me? Right up from the field, with the representatives of three colleges standing by? And the buyers I brought, and the cheers when he came out—Loman, Loman, Loman! God Almighty, he'll be great yet. A star like that, magnificent, can never really fade away!

The light on **Willy** *is fading. The gas heater begins to glow through the kitchen wall, near the stairs, a blue flame beneath red coils.*

Linda (*timidly*) Willy dear, what has he got against you?

Willy I'm so tired. Don't talk any more.

Biff *slowly returns to the kitchen. He stops, stares toward the heater.*

Linda Will you ask Howard to let you work in New York?

Willy First thing in the morning. Everything'll be all right.

Biff *reaches behind the heater and draws out a length of rubber tubing. He is horrified and turns his head toward* **Willy***'s room, still dimly lit, from which the strains of* **Linda***'s desperate but monotonous humming rise.*

Willy (*staring through the window into the moonlight*) Gee, look at the moon moving between the buildings!

Biff *wraps the tubing around his hand and quickly goes up the stairs.*

Curtain.

Act Two

Music is heard, gay and bright. The curtain rises as the music fades away. **Willy**, *in shirt sleeves, is sitting at the kitchen table, sipping coffee, his hat in his lap.* **Linda** *is filling his cup when she can.*

Willy Wonderful coffee. Meal in itself.

Linda Can I make you some eggs?

Willy No. Take a breath.

Linda You look so rested, dear.

Willy I slept like a dead one. First time in months. Imagine, sleeping till ten on a Tuesday morning. Boys left nice and early, heh?

Linda They were out of here by eight o'clock.

Willy Good work!

Linda It was so thrilling to see them leaving together. I can't get over the shaving lotion in this house!

Willy (*smiling*) Mmm—

Linda Biff was very changed this morning. His whole attitude seemed to be hopeful. He couldn't wait to get downtown to see Oliver.

Willy He's heading for a change. There's no question, there simply are certain men that take longer to get—solidified. How did he dress?

Linda His blue suit. He's so handsome in that suit. He could be a—anything in that suit!

Willy *gets up from the table.* **Linda** *holds his jacket for him.*

Willy There's no question, no question at all. Gee, on the way home tonight I'd like to buy some seeds.

Linda (*laughing*) That'd be wonderful. But not enough sun gets back there. Nothing'll grow any more.

Willy You wait, kid, before it's all over we're gonna get a little place out in the country, and I'll raise some vegetables, a couple of chickens . . .

Linda You'll do it yet, dear.

Willy *walks out of his jacket.* **Linda** *follows him.*

Willy And they'll get married, and come for a weekend. I'd build a little guest house. 'Cause I got so many fine tools, all I'd need would be a little lumber and some peace of mind.

Linda (*joyfully*) I sewed the lining . . .

Willy I could build two guest houses, so they'd both come. Did he decide how much he's going to ask Oliver for?

Linda (*getting him into the jacket*) He didn't mention it, but I imagine ten or fifteen thousand. You going to talk to Howard today?

Willy Yeah. I'll put it to him straight and simple. He'll just have to take me off the road.

Linda And Willy, don't forget to ask for a little advance, because we've got the insurance premium. It's the grace period now.

Willy That's a hundred . . .?

Linda A hundred and eight, sixty-eight. Because we're a little short again.

Willy Why are we short?

Linda Well, you had the motor job on the car . . .

Willy That goddam Studebaker!

Linda And you got one more payment on the refrigerator . . .

Willy But it just broke again!

Linda Well, it's old, dear.

Willy I told you we should've bought a well-advertised machine. Charley bought a General Electric and it's twenty years old and it's still good, that son-of-a-bitch.

Linda But, Willy—

Willy Whoever heard of a Hastings refrigerator? Once in my life I would like to own something outright before it's broken! I'm always in a race with the junkyard! I just finished paying for the car and it's on its last legs. The refrigerator consumes belts like a goddam maniac. They time those things. They time them so when you finally paid for them, they're used up.

Linda (*buttoning up his jacket as he unbuttons it*) All told, about two hundred dollars would carry us, dear. But that includes the last payment on the mortgage. After this payment, Willy, the house belongs to us.

Willy It's twenty-five years!

Linda Biff was nine years old when we bought it.

Willy Well, that's a great thing. To weather a twenty-five-year mortgage is—

Linda It's an accomplishment.

Willy All the cement, the lumber, the reconstruction I put in this house! There ain't a crack to be found in it any more.

Linda Well, it served its purpose.

Willy What purpose? Some stranger'll come along, move in, and that's that. If only Biff would take this house, and raise a family . . . (*He starts to go.*) Good-by, I'm late.

Linda (*suddenly remembering*) Oh, I forgot! You're supposed to meet them for dinner.

Willy Me?

Linda At Frank's Chop House on Forty-eighth near Sixth Avenue.

Willy Is that so! How about you?

Linda No, just the three of you. They're gonna blow you to a big meal!

Willy Don't say! Who thought of that?

Linda Biff came to me this morning, Willy, and he said, "Tell Dad, we want to blow him to a big meal." Be there six o'clock. You and your two boys are going to have dinner.

Willy Gee whiz! That's really somethin'. I'm gonna knock Howard for a loop, kid. I'll get an advance, and I'll come home with a New York job. Goddammit, now I'm gonna do it!

Linda Oh, that's the spirit, Willy!

Willy I will never get behind a wheel the rest of my life!

Linda It's changing, Willy, I can feel it changing!

Willy Beyond a question. G'by, I'm late. (*He starts to go again.*)

Linda (*calling after him as she runs to the kitchen table for a handkerchief*) You got your glasses?

Willy (*feels for them, then comes back in*) Yeah, yeah, got my glasses.

Linda (*giving him the handkerchief*) And a handkerchief.

Willy Yeah, handkerchief.

Linda And your saccharine?

Willy Yeah, my saccharine.

Linda Be careful on the subway stairs.

She kisses him, and a silk stocking is seen hanging from her hand. **Willy** *notices it.*

Willy Will you stop mending stockings? At least while I'm in the house. It gets me nervous. I can't tell you. Please.

Linda *hides the stocking in her hand as she follows* **Willy** *across the forestage in front of the house.*

Linda Remember, Frank's Chop House.

Willy (*passing the apron*) Maybe beets would grow out there.

Linda (*laughing*) But you tried so many times.

Willy Yeah. Well, don't work hard today. (*He disappears around the right corner of the house.*)

Linda Be careful!

As **Willy** *vanishes,* **Linda** *waves to him. Suddenly the phone rings. She runs across the stage and into the kitchen and lifts it.*

Linda Hello? Oh, Biff! I'm so glad you called, I just . . . Yes, sure, I just told him. Yes, he'll be there for dinner at six o'clock, I didn't forget. Listen, I was just dying to tell you. You know that little rubber pipe I told you about? That he connected to the gas heater? I finally decided to go down the cellar this morning and take it away and destroy it. But it's gone! Imagine? He took it away himself, it isn't there! (*She listens.*) When? Oh, then you took it. Oh—nothing, it's just that I'd hoped he'd taken it away himself. Oh, I'm not worried, darling, because this morning he left in such high spirits, it was like the old days! I'm not afraid any more. Did Mr. Oliver see you? . . . Well, you wait there then. And make a nice impression on him, darling. Just don't perspire too much before you see him. And have a nice time with Dad. He may have big news too! . . . That's right, a New York job. And be sweet to him tonight, dear. Be loving to him. Because he's only a little boat looking for a harbor. (*She is trembling with sorrow and joy.*) Oh, that's wonderful, Biff, you'll save his life. Thanks, darling. Just put your arm around him when he comes into the restaurant. Give him a smile. That's the boy . . . Good-by, dear. . . . You got your comb? . . . That's fine. Good-by, Biff dear.

In the middle of her speech, **Howard Wagner**, *thirty-six, wheels on a small typewriter table on which is a wire-recording machine and proceeds to plug it in. This is on the left forestage. Light slowly fades on* **Linda** *as it rises on* **Howard**. **Howard** *is intent on threading the machine and only glances over his shoulder as* **Willy** *appears.*

Willy Pst! Pst!

Howard Hello, Willy, come in.

Willy Like to have a little talk with you, Howard.

Howard Sorry to keep you waiting. I'll be with you in a minute.

Willy What's that, Howard?

Howard Didn't you ever see one of these? Wire recorder.

Willy Oh. Can we talk a minute?

Howard Records things. Just got delivery yesterday. Been driving me crazy, the most terrific machine I ever saw in my life. I was up all night with it.

Willy What do you do with it?

Howard I bought it for dictation, but you can do anything with it. Listen to this. I had it home last night. Listen to what I picked up. The first one is my daughter. Get this. (*He flicks the switch and "Roll out the Barrel" is heard being whistled.*) Listen to that kid whistle.

Willy That is lifelike, isn't it?

Howard Seven years old. Get that tone.

Willy Ts, ts. Like to ask a little favor if you . . .

The whistling breaks off, and the voice of **Howard***'s daughter is heard.*

His Daughter "Now you, Daddy."

Howard She's crazy for me! (*Again the same song is whistled.*) That's me! Ha! (*He winks.*)

Willy You're very good!

The whistling breaks off again. The machine runs silent for a moment.

Howard Sh! Get this now, this is my son.

His Son "The capital of Alabama is Montgomery; the capital of Arizona is Phoenix; the capital of Arkansas is Little Rock; the capital of California is Sacramento . . ." (*and on, and on.*)

Howard (*holding up five fingers*) Five years old, Willy!

Willy He'll make an announcer some day!

His Son (*continuing*) "The capital . . ."

Howard Get that—alphabetical order! (*The machine breaks off suddenly.*) Wait a minute. The maid kicked the plug out.

Willy It certainly is a—

Howard Sh, for God's sake!

His Son "It's nine o'clock, Bulova watch time. So I have to go to sleep."

Willy That really is—

Howard Wait a minute! The next is my wife.

They wait.

Howard's Voice "Go on, say something." (*Pause.*) "Well, you gonna talk?"

His Wife "I can't think of anything."

Howard's Voice "Well, talk—it's turning."

His Wife (*shyly, beaten*) "Hello." (*Silence.*) "Oh, Howard, I can't talk into this . . ."

Howard (*snapping the machine off*) That was my wife.

Willy That is a wonderful machine. Can we—

Howard I tell you, Willy, I'm gonna take my camera, and my bandsaw, and all my hobbies, and out they go. This is the most fascinating relaxation I ever found.

Willy I think I'll get one myself.

Howard Sure, they're only a hundred and a half. You can't do without it. Supposing you wanna hear Jack Benny, see? But you can't be at home at that hour. So you tell the maid to turn the radio on when Jack Benny comes on, and this automatically goes on with the radio . . .

Willy And when you come home you . . .

Howard You can come home twelve o'clock, one o'clock, any time you like, and you get yourself a Coke and sit yourself down, throw the switch, and there's Jack Benny's program in the middle of the night!

Willy I'm definitely going to get one. Because lots of time I'm on the road, and I think to myself, what I must be missing on the radio!

Howard Don't you have a radio in the car?

Willy Well, yeah, but who ever thinks of turning it on?

Howard Say, aren't you supposed to be in Boston?

Willy That's what I want to talk to you about, Howard. You got a minute? (*He draws a chair in from the wing.*)

Howard What happened? What're you doing here?

Willy Well . . .

Howard You didn't crack up again, did you?

Willy Oh, no. No . . .

Howard Geez, you had me worried there for a minute. What's the trouble?

Willy Well, tell you the truth, Howard. I've come to the decision that I'd rather not travel any more.

Howard Not travel! Well, what'll you do?

Willy Remember, Christmas time, when you had the party here? You said you'd try to think of some spot for me here in town.

Howard With us?

Willy Well, sure.

Howard Oh, yeah, yeah. I remember. Well, I couldn't think of anything for you, Willy.

Willy I tell ya, Howard. The kids are all grown up, y'know. I don't need much any more. If I could take home—well, sixty-five dollars a week, I could swing it.

Howard Yeah, but Willy, see I—

Willy I tell ya why, Howard. Speaking frankly and between the two of us, y'know—I'm just a little tired.

Howard Oh, I could understand that, Willy. But you're a road man, Willy, and we do a road business. We've only got a half-dozen salesmen on the floor here.

Willy God knows, Howard, I never asked a favor of any man. But I was with the firm when your father used to carry you in here in his arms.

Howard I know that, Willy, but—

Willy Your father came to me the day you were born and asked me what I thought of the name of Howard, may he rest in peace.

Howard I appreciate that, Willy, but there just is no spot here for you. If I had a spot I'd slam you right in, but I just don't have a single solitary spot.

He looks for his lighter. **Willy** *has picked it up and gives it to him. Pause.*

Willy (*with increasing anger*) Howard, all I need to set my table is fifty dollars a week.

Howard But where am I going to put you, kid?

Willy Look, it isn't a question of whether I can sell merchandise, is it?

Howard No, but it's a business, kid, and everybody's gotta pull his own weight.

Willy (*desperately*) Just let me tell you a story, Howard—

Howard 'Cause you gotta admit, business is business.

Willy (*angrily*) Business is definitely business, but just listen for a minute. You don't understand this. When I was a boy—eighteen, nineteen—I was already on the road. And there was a question in my mind as to whether selling had a future for me. Because in those days I had a yearning to go to Alaska. See, there were three gold strikes in one month in Alaska, and I felt like going out. Just for the ride, you might say.

Howard (*barely interested*) Don't say.

Willy Oh, yeah, my father lived many years in Alaska. He was an adventurous man. We've got quite a little streak of self-reliance in our family. I thought I'd go out with my older brother and try to locate him, and maybe settle in the North with the old man. And I was almost decided to go, when I met a salesman in the Parker House. His name was Dave Singleman. And he was eighty-four years old, and he'd drummed merchandise in thirty-one states. And old Dave, he'd go up to his room, y'understand, put on his green velvet slippers—I'll never forget—and pick up his phone and call the buyers, and without ever leaving his room, at the age of eighty-four, he made his living. And when I saw that, I realized that selling was the greatest career a man could want. 'Cause what could be more satisfying than to be able to go, at the age of eighty-four, into twenty or thirty different cities, and pick up a phone, and be remembered and loved and helped by so many different people? Do you know? when he died—and by the way he died the death of a salesman, in his green velvet slippers in the smoker of the New York, New Haven and Hartford, going into Boston—when he died, hundreds of salesmen and buyers were at his funeral. Things were sad on a lotta trains for months after that. (*He stands up.* **Howard** *has not looked at him.*) In those days there was personality in it, Howard. There was respect, and comradeship, and gratitude in it. Today, it's all cut and dried, and there's no chance for bringing friendship to bear—or personality. You see what I mean? They don't know me any more.

Howard (*moving away, toward the right*) That's just the thing, Willy.

Willy If I had forty dollars a week—that's all I'd need. Forty dollars, Howard.

Howard Kid, I can't take blood from a stone, I—

Willy (*desperation is on him now*) Howard, the year Al Smith was nominated, your father came to me and—

Howard (*starting to go off*) I've got to see some people, kid.

Willy (*stopping him*) I'm talking about your father! There were promises made across this desk! You mustn't tell me you've got people to see—I put thirty-four years into this firm, Howard, and now I can't pay my insurance! You can't eat the orange and throw the peel away—a man is not a piece of fruit! (*After a pause:*) Now pay attention. Your father—in 1928 I had a big year. I averaged a hundred and seventy dollars a week in commissions.

Howard (*impatiently*) Now, Willy, you never averaged—

Willy (*banging his hand on the desk*) I averaged a hundred and seventy dollars a week in the year of 1928! And your father came to me—or rather, I was in the office here—it was right over this desk—and he put his hand on my shoulder—

Howard (*getting up*) You'll have to excuse me, Willy, I gotta see some people. Pull yourself together. (*Going out:*) I'll be back in a little while.

On **Howard***'s exit, the light on his chair grows very bright and strange.*

Willy Pull myself together! What the hell did I say to him? My God, I was yelling at him! How could I! (**Willy** *breaks off, staring at the light, which occupies the chair, animating it. He approaches this chair, standing across the desk from it.*) Frank, Frank, don't you remember what you told me that time? How you put your hand on my shoulder, and Frank . . . (*He leans on the desk and as he speaks the dead man's name he accidentally switches on the recorder, and instantly*)

Howard's Son ". . . of New York is Albany. The capital of Ohio is Cincinnati, the capital of Rhode Island is . . ." (*The recitation continues.*)

Willy (*leaping away with fright, shouting*) Ha! Howard! Howard! Howard!

Howard (*rushing in*) What happened?

Willy (*pointing at the machine, which continues nasally, childishly, with the capital cities*) Shut it off! Shut it off!

Howard (*pulling the plug out*) Look, Willy . . .

Willy (*pressing his hands to his eyes*) I gotta get myself some coffee. I'll get some coffee . . .

Willy *starts to walk out.* **Howard** *stops him.*

Howard (*rolling up the cord*) Willy, look . . .

Willy I'll go to Boston.

Howard Willy, you can't go to Boston for us.

Willy Why can't I go?

Howard I don't want you to represent us. I've been meaning to tell you for a long time now.

Willy Howard, are you firing me?

Howard I think you need a good long rest, Willy.

Willy Howard—

Howard And when you feel better, come back, and we'll see if we can work something out.

Willy But I gotta earn money, Howard. I'm in no position to—

Howard Where are your sons? Why don't your sons give you a hand?

Willy They're working on a very big deal.

Howard This is no time for false pride, Willy. You go to your sons and you tell them that you're tired. You've got two great boys, haven't you?

Willy Oh, no question, no question, but in the meantime . . .

Howard Then that's that, heh?

Willy All right, I'll go to Boston tomorrow.

Howard No, no.

Willy I can't throw myself on my sons. I'm not a cripple!

Howard Look, kid, I'm busy this morning.

Willy (*grasping* **Howard**'*s arm*) Howard, you've got to let me go to Boston!

Howard (*hard, keeping himself under control*) I've got a line of people to see this morning. Sit down, take five minutes, and pull yourself together, and then go home, will ya? I need the office, Willy. (*He starts to go, turns, remembering the recorder, starts to push off the table holding the recorder.*) Oh, yeah. Whenever you can this week, stop by and drop off the samples. You'll feel better, Willy, and then come back and we'll talk. Pull yourself together, kid, there's people outside.

Howard *exits, pushing the table off left.* **Willy** *stares into space, exhausted. Now the music is heard—***Ben**'*s music—first distantly, then closer, closer. As* **Willy** *speaks,* **Ben** *enters from the right. He carries valise and umbrella.*

Willy Oh, Ben, how did you do it? What is the answer? Did you wind up the Alaska deal already?

Ben Doesn't take much time if you know what you're doing. Just a short business trip. Boarding ship in an hour. Wanted to say good-by.

Willy Ben, I've got to talk to you.

Ben (*glancing at his watch*) Haven't the time, William.

Willy (*crossing the apron to* **Ben**) Ben, nothing's working out. I don't know what to do.

Ben Now, look here, William. I've bought timberland in Alaska and I need a man to look after things for me.

Willy God, timberland! Me and my boys in those grand outdoors!

Ben You've a new continent at your doorstep, William. Get out of these cities, they're full of talk and time payments and courts of law. Screw on your fists and you can fight for a fortune up there.

Willy Yes, yes! Linda, Linda!

Linda *enters as of old, with the wash.*

Linda Oh, you're back?

Ben I haven't much time.

Willy No, wait! Linda, he's got a proposition for me in Alaska.

Linda But you've got— (*To* **Ben**:) He's got a beautiful job here.

Willy But in Alaska, kid, I could—

Linda You're doing well enough, Willy!

Ben (*to* **Linda**) Enough for what, my dear?

Linda (*frightened of* **Ben** *and angry at him*) Don't say those things to him! Enough to be happy right here, right now. (*To* **Willy**, *while* **Ben** *laughs:*) Why must everybody conquer the world? You're well liked, and the boys love you, and someday (*to* **Ben**:) why, old man Wagner told him just the other day that if he keeps it up he'll be a member of the firm, didn't he, Willy?

Willy Sure, sure. I am building something with this firm, Ben, and if a man is building something he must be on the right track, mustn't he?

Ben What are you building? Lay your hand on it. Where is it?

Willy (*hesitantly*) That's true, Linda, there's nothing.

Linda Why? (*To* **Ben**:) There's a man eighty-four years old—

Willy That's right, Ben, that's right. When I look at that man I say, what is there to worry about?

Ben Bah!

Willy It's true, Ben. All he has to do is go into any city, pick up the phone, and he's making his living and you know why?

Ben (*picking up his valise*) I've got to go.

Willy (*holding* **Ben** *back*) Look at this boy!

Biff, *in his high school sweater, enters carrying suitcase.* **Happy** *carries* **Biff***'s shoulder guards, gold helmet, and football pants.*

Willy Without a penny to his name, three great universities are begging for him, and from there the sky's the limit, because it's not what you do, Ben. It's who you know and the smile on your face! It's contacts, Ben, contacts! The whole wealth of Alaska passes over the lunch table at the Commodore Hotel, and that's the wonder, the wonder of this country, that a man can end with diamonds here on the basis of being liked! (*He turns to* **Biff**.) And that's why when you get out on that field today it's important. Because thousands of people will be rooting for you and loving you. (*To* **Ben**, *who has again begun to leave:*) And Ben! when he walks into a business office his name will sound out like a bell and all the doors will open to him! I've seen it, Ben, I've seen it a thousand times! You can't feel it with your hand like timber, but it's there!

Ben Good-by, William.

Willy Ben, am I right? Don't you think I'm right? I value your advice.

Ben There's a new continent at your doorstep, William. You could walk out rich. Rich! (*He is gone.*)

Willy We'll do it here, Ben! You hear me? We're gonna do it here!

Young Bernard *rushes in. The gay music of the boys is heard.*

Bernard Oh, gee, I was afraid you left already!

Willy Why? What time is it?

Bernard It's half-past one!

Willy Well, come on, everybody! Ebbets Field next stop! Where's the pennants? (*He rushes through the wall-line of the kitchen and out into the living-room.*)

Linda (*to* **Biff**) Did you pack fresh underwear?

Biff (*who has been limbering up*) I want to go!

Bernard Biff, I'm carrying your helmet, ain't I?

Happy No, I'm carrying the helmet.

Bernard Oh, Biff, you promised me.

Happy I'm carrying the helmet.

Bernard How am I going to get in the locker room?

Linda Let him carry the shoulder guards. (*She puts her coat and hat on in the kitchen.*)

Bernard Can I, Biff? 'Cause I told everybody I'm going to be in the locker room.

Happy In Ebbets Field it's the clubhouse.

Bernard I meant the clubhouse. Biff!

Happy Biff!

Biff (*grandly, after a slight pause*) Let him carry the shoulder guards.

Happy (*as he gives* **Bernard** *the shoulder guards*) Stay close to us now.

Willy *rushes in with the pennants.*

Willy (*handing them out*) Everybody wave when Biff comes out on the field. (**Happy** *and* **Bernard** *run off.*) You set now, boy?

The music has died away.

Biff Ready to go, Pop. Every muscle is ready.

Willy (*at the edge of the apron*) You realize what this means?

Biff That's right, Pop.

Willy (*feeling* **Biff***'s muscles*) You're comin' home this afternoon captain of the All-Scholastic Championship Team of the City of New York.

Biff I got it, Pop. And remember, pal, when I take off my helmet, that touchdown is for you.

Willy Let's go! (*He is starting out, with his arm around* **Biff***, when* **Charley** *enters, as of old, in knickers.*) I got no room for you, Charley.

Charley Room? For what?

Willy In the car.

Charley You goin' for a ride? I wanted to shoot some casino.

Willy (*furiously*) Casino! (*Incredulously:*) Don't you realize what today is?

Linda Oh, he knows, Willy. He's just kidding you.

Willy That's nothing to kid about!

Charley No, Linda, what's goin' on?

Linda He's playing in Ebbets Field.

Charley Baseball in this weather?

Willy Don't talk to him. Come on, come on! (*He is pushing them out.*)

Charley Wait a minute, didn't you hear the news?

Willy What?

Charley Don't you listen to the radio? Ebbets Field just blew up.

Willy You go to hell! (**Charley** *laughs. Pushing them out:*) Come on, come on! We're late.

Charley (*as they go*) Knock a homer, Biff, knock a homer!

Willy (*the last to leave, turning to* **Charley**) I don't think that was funny, Charley. This is the greatest day of his life.

Charley Willy, when are you going to grow up?

Willy Yeah, heh? When this game is over, Charley, you'll be laughing out of the other side of your face. They'll be calling him another Red Grange. Twenty-five thousand a year.

Charley (*kidding*) Is that so?

Willy Yeah, that's so.

Charley Well, then, I'm sorry, Willy. But tell me something.

Willy What?

Charley Who is Red Grange?

Willy Put up your hands. Goddam you, put up your hands!

Charley, *chuckling, shakes his head and walks away, around the left corner of the stage.* **Willy** *follows him. The music rises to a mocking frenzy.*

Willy Who the hell do you think you are, better than everybody else? You don't know everything, you big, ignorant, stupid . . . Put up your hands!

Light rises, on the right side of the forestage, on a small table in the reception room of **Charley***'s office. Traffic sounds are heard.* **Bernard**, *now mature, sits whistling to himself. A pair of tennis rackets and an overnight bag are on the floor beside him.*

Willy (*offstage*) What are you walking away for? Don't walk away! If you're going to say something say it to my face! I know you laugh at me behind my back. You'll laugh out of the other side of your goddam face after this game. Touchdown! Touchdown! Eighty thousand people! Touchdown! Right between the goal posts.

Bernard *is a quiet, earnest, but self-assured young man.* **Willy***'s voice is coming from right upstage now.* **Bernard** *lowers his feet off the table and listens.* **Jenny**, *his father's secretary, enters.*

Jenny (*distressed*) Say, Bernard, will you go out in the hall?

Bernard What is that noise? Who is it?

Jenny Mr. Loman. He just got off the elevator.

Bernard (*getting up*) Who's he arguing with?

Jenny Nobody. There's nobody with him. I can't deal with him any more, and your father gets all upset everytime he comes. I've got a lot of typing to do, and your father's waiting to sign it. Will you see him?

Willy (*entering*) Touchdown! Touch—(*He sees* **Jenny**.) Jenny, Jenny, good to see you. How're ya? Workin'? Or still honest?

Jenny Fine. How've you been feeling?

Willy Not much any more, Jenny. Ha, ha! (*He is surprised to see the rackets.*)

Bernard Hello, Uncle Willy.

Willy (*almost shocked*) Bernard! Well, look who's here! (*He comes quickly, guiltily, to* **Bernard** *and warmly shakes his hand.*)

Bernard How are you? Good to see you.

Willy What are you doing here?

Bernard Oh, just stopped by to see Pop. Get off my feet till my train leaves. I'm going to Washington in a few minutes.

Willy Is he in?

Bernard Yes, he's in his office with the accountant. Sit down.

Willy (*sitting down*) What're you going to do in Washington?

Bernard Oh, just a case I've got there, Willy.

Willy That so? (*Indicating the rackets:*) You going to play tennis there?

Bernard I'm staying with a friend who's got a court.

Willy Don't say. His own tennis court. Must be fine people, I bet.

Bernard They are, very nice. Dad tells me Biff's in town.

Willy (*with a big smile*) Yeah, Biff's in. Working on a very big deal, Bernard.

Bernard What's Biff doing?

Willy Well, he's been doing very big things in the West. But he decided to establish himself here. Very big. We're having dinner. Did I hear your wife had a boy?

Bernard That's right. Our second.

Willy Two boys! What do you know!

Bernard What kind of a deal has Biff got?

Willy Well, Bill Oliver—very big sporting-goods man—he wants Biff very badly. Called him in from the West. Long distance, carte blanche, special deliveries. Your friends have their own private tennis court?

Bernard You still with the old firm, Willy?

Willy (*after a pause*) I'm—I'm overjoyed to see how you made the grade, Bernard, overjoyed. It's an encouraging thing to see a young man really—really—Looks very good for Biff—very—(*He breaks off, then:*) Bernard—(*He is so full of emotion, he breaks off again.*)

Bernard What is it, Willy?

Willy (*small and alone*) What—what's the secret?

Bernard What secret?

Willy How—how did you? Why didn't he ever catch on?

Bernard I wouldn't know that, Willy.

Willy (*confidentially, desperately*) You were his friend, his boyhood friend. There's something I don't understand about it. His life ended after that Ebbets Field game. From the age of seventeen nothing good ever happened to him.

Bernard He never trained himself for anything.

Willy But he did, he did. After high school he took so many correspondence courses. Radio mechanics; television; God knows what, and never made the slightest mark.

Bernard (*taking off his glasses*) Willy, do you want to talk candidly?

Willy (*rising, faces* **Bernard**) I regard you as a very brilliant man, Bernard. I value your advice.

Bernard Oh, the hell with the advice, Willy. I couldn't advise you. There's just one thing I've always wanted to ask you. When he was supposed to graduate, and the math teacher flunked him—

Willy Oh, that son-of-a-bitch ruined his life.

Bernard Yeah, but, Willy, all he had to do was go to summer school and make up that subject.

Willy That's right, that's right.

Bernard Did you tell him not to go to summer school?

Willy Me? I begged him to go. I ordered him to go!

Bernard Then why wouldn't he go?

Willy Why? Why! Bernard, that question has been trailing me like a ghost for the last fifteen years. He flunked the subject, and laid down and died like a hammer hit him!

Bernard Take it easy, kid.

Willy Let me talk to you—I got nobody to talk to. Bernard, Bernard, was it my fault? Y'see? It keeps going around in my mind, maybe I did something to him. I got nothing to give him.

Bernard Don't take it so hard.

Willy Why did he lay down? What is the story there? You were his friend!

Bernard Willy, I remember, it was June, and our grades came out. And he'd flunked math.

Willy That son-of-a-bitch!

Bernard No, it wasn't right then. Biff just got very angry, I remember, and he was ready to enroll in summer school.

Willy (*surprised*) He was?

Bernard He wasn't beaten by it at all. But then, Willy, he disappeared from the block for almost a month. And I got the idea that he'd gone up to New England to see you. Did he have a talk with you then?

Willy *stares in silence.*

Bernard Willy?

Willy (*with a strong edge of resentment in his voice*) Yeah, he came to Boston. What about it?

Bernard Well, just that when he came back—I'll never forget this, it always mystifies me. Because I'd thought so well of Biff, even though he'd always taken advantage of me. I loved him, Willy, y'know? And he came back after that month and took his sneakers—remember those sneakers with "University of Virginia" printed on them? He was so proud of those, wore them every day. And he took them down in the cellar, and burned them up in the furnace. We had a fist fight. It lasted at least half an hour. Just the two of us, punching each other down the cellar, and crying right through it. I've often thought of how strange it was that I knew he'd given up his life. What happened in Boston, Willy?

Willy *looks at him as at an intruder.*

Bernard I just bring it up because you asked me.

Willy (*angrily*) Nothing. What do you mean, "What happened?" What's that got to do with anything?

Bernard Well, don't get sore.

Willy What are you trying to do, blame it on me? If a boy lays down is that my fault?

Bernard Now, Willy, don't get—

Willy Well, don't—don't talk to me that way! What does that mean, "What happened?"

Charley *enters. He is in his vest, and he carries a bottle of bourbon.*

Charley Hey, you're going to miss that train. (*He waves the bottle.*)

Bernard Yeah, I'm going. (*He takes the bottle.*) Thanks, Pop. (*He picks up his rackets and bag.*) Good-by, Willy, and don't worry about it. You know, "If at first you don't succeed . . ."

Willy Yes, I believe in that.

Bernard But sometimes, Willy, it's better for a man just to walk away.

Willy Walk away?

Bernard That's right.

Willy But if you can't walk away?

Bernard (*after a slight pause*) I guess that's when it's tough. (*Extending his hand:*) Good-by, Willy.

Willy (*shaking* **Bernard***'s hand*) Good-by, boy.

Charley (*an arm on* **Bernard***'s shoulder*) How do you like this kid? Gonna argue a case in front of the Supreme Court.

Bernard (*protesting*) Pop!

Willy (*genuinely shocked, pained, and happy*) No! The Supreme Court!

Bernard I gotta run. 'By, Dad!

Charley Knock 'em dead, Bernard!

Bernard *goes off.*

Willy (*as* **Charley** *takes out his wallet*) The Supreme Court! And he didn't even mention it!

Charley (*counting out money on the desk*) He don't have to—he's gonna do it.

Willy And you never told him what to do, did you? You never took any interest in him.

Charley My salvation is that I never took any interest in anything. There's some money—fifty dollars. I got an accountant inside.

Willy Charley, look . . . (*With difficulty:*) I got my insurance to pay. If you can manage it—I need a hundred and ten dollars.

Charley *doesn't reply for a moment; merely stops moving.*

Willy I'd draw it from my bank but Linda would know, and I . . .

Charley Sit down, Willy.

Willy (*moving toward the chair*) I'm keeping an account of everything, remember. I'll pay every penny back. (*He sits.*)

Charley Now listen to me, Willy.

Willy I want you to know I appreciate . . .

Charley (*sitting down on the table*) Willy, what're you doin'? What the hell is goin' on in your head?

Willy Why? I'm simply . . .

Charley I offered you a job. You can make fifty dollars a week. And I won't send you on the road.

Willy I've got a job.

Charley Without pay? What kind of a job is a job without pay? (*He rises.*) Now, look, kid, enough is enough. I'm no genius but I know when I'm being insulted.

Willy Insulted!

Charley Why don't you want to work for me?

Willy What's the matter with you? I've got a job.

Charley Then what're you walkin' in here every week for?

Willy (*getting up*) Well, if you don't want me to walk in here—

Charley I am offering you a job.

Willy I don't want your goddam job!

Charley When the hell are you going to grow up?

Willy (*furiously*) You big ignoramus, if you say that to me again I'll rap you one! I don't care how big you are! (*He's ready to fight.*)

Pause.

Charley (*kindly, going to him*) How much do you need, Willy?

Willy Charley, I'm strapped, I'm strapped. I don't know what to do. I was just fired.

Charley Howard fired you?

Willy That snotnose. Imagine that? I named him. I named him Howard.

Charley Willy, when're you gonna realize that them things don't mean anything? You named him Howard, but you can't sell that. The only thing you got in this world is what you can sell. And the funny thing is that you're a salesman, and you don't know that.

Willy I've always tried to think otherwise, I guess. I always felt that if a man was impressive, and well liked, that nothing—

Charley Why must everybody like you? Who liked J. P. Morgan? Was he impressive? In a Turkish bath he'd look like a butcher. But with his pockets on he was very well liked. Now listen, Willy, I know you don't like me, and nobody can say I'm in love with you, but I'll give you a job because—just for the hell of it, put it that way. Now what do you say?

Willy I—I just can't work for you, Charley.

Charley What're you, jealous of me?

Willy I can't work for you, that's all, don't ask me why.

Charley (*angered, takes out more bills*) You been jealous of me all your life, you damned fool! Here, pay your insurance. (*He puts the money in* **Willy***'s hand.*)

Willy I'm keeping strict accounts.

Charley I've got some work to do. Take care of yourself. And pay your insurance.

Willy (*moving to the right*) Funny, y'know? After all the highways, and the trains, and the appointments, and the years, you end up worth more dead than alive.

Charley Willy, nobody's worth nothin' dead. (*After a slight pause:*) Did you hear what I said?

Willy *stands still, dreaming.*

Charley Willy!

Willy Apologize to Bernard for me when you see him. I didn't mean to argue with him. He's a fine boy. They're all fine boys, and they'll end up big—all of them. Someday they'll all play tennis together. Wish me luck, Charley. He saw Bill Oliver today.

Charley Good luck.

Willy (*on the verge of tears*) Charley, you're the only friend I got. Isn't that a remarkable thing? (*He goes out.*)

Charley Jesus!

Charley *stares after him a moment and follows. All light blacks out. Suddenly raucous music is heard, and a red glow rises behind the screen at right.* **Stanley***, a young waiter, appears, carrying a table, followed by* **Happy***, who is carrying two chairs.*

Stanley (*putting the table down*) That's all right, Mr. Loman, I can handle it myself. (*He turns and takes the chairs from* **Happy** *and places them at the table.*)

Happy (*glancing around*) Oh, this is better.

Stanley Sure, in the front there you're in the middle of all kinds a noise. Whenever you got a party, Mr. Loman, you just tell me and I'll put you back here. Y'know, there's a lotta people they don't like it private, because when they go out they like to see a lotta action around them because they're sick and tired to stay in the house by theirself. But I know you, you ain't from Hackensack. You know what I mean?

Happy (*sitting down*) So how's it coming, Stanley?

Stanley Ah, it's a dog's life. I only wish during the war they'd a took me in the Army. I coulda been dead by now.

Happy My brother's back, Stanley.

Stanley Oh, he come back, heh? From the Far West.

Happy Yeah, big cattle man, my brother, so treat him right. And my father's coming too.

Stanley Oh, your father too!

Happy You got a couple of nice lobsters?

Stanley Hundred per cent, big.

Happy I want them with the claws.

Stanley Don't worry, I don't give you no mice. (**Happy** *laughs.*) How about some wine? It'll put a head on the meal.

Happy No. You remember, Stanley, that recipe I brought you from overseas? With the champagne in it?

Stanley Oh, yeah, sure. I still got it tacked up yet in the kitchen. But that'll have to cost a buck apiece anyways.

Happy That's all right.

Stanley What'd you, hit a number or somethin'?

Happy No, it's a little celebration. My brother is—I think he pulled off a big deal today. I think we're going into business together.

Stanley Great! That's the best for you. Because a family business, you know what I mean?—that's the best.

Happy That's what I think.

Stanley 'Cause what's the difference? Somebody steals? It's in the family. Know what I mean? (*Sotto voce:*) Like this bartender here. The boss is goin' crazy what kinda leak he's got in the cash register. You put it in but it don't come out.

Happy (*raising his head*) Sh!

Stanley What?

Happy You notice I wasn't lookin' right or left, was I?

Stanley No.

Happy And my eyes are closed.

Stanley So what's the—?

Happy Strudel's comin'.

Stanley (*catching on, looks around*) Ah, no, there's no—

He breaks off as a furred, lavishly dressed girl enters and sits at the next table. Both follow her with their eyes.

Stanley Geez, how'd ya know?

Happy I got radar or something. (*Staring directly at her profile:*) Oooooooo . . . Stanley.

Stanley I think that's for you, Mr. Loman.

Happy Look at that mouth. Oh, God. And the binoculars.

Stanley Geez, you got a life, Mr. Loman.

Happy Wait on her.

Stanley (*going to the girl's table*) Would you like a menu, ma'am?

Girl I'm expecting someone, but I'd like a—

Happy Why don't you bring her—excuse me, miss, do you mind? I sell champagne, and I'd like you to try my brand. Bring her a champagne, Stanley.

Girl That's awfully nice of you.

Happy Don't mention it. It's all company money. (*He laughs.*)

Girl That's a charming product to be selling, isn't it?

Happy Oh, gets to be like everything else. Selling is selling, y'know.

Girl I suppose.

Happy You don't happen to sell, do you?

Girl No, I don't sell.

Happy Would you object to a compliment from a stranger? You ought to be on a magazine cover.

Girl (*looking at him a little archly*) I have been.

Stanley *comes in with a glass of champagne.*

Happy What'd I say before, Stanley? You see? She's a cover girl.

Stanley Oh, I could see, I could see.

Happy (*to the* **Girl**) What magazine?

Girl Oh, a lot of them. (*She takes the drink.*) Thank you.

Happy You know what they say in France, don't you? "Champagne is the drink of the complexion"—Hya, Biff!

Biff *has entered and sits with* **Happy**.

Biff Hello, kid. Sorry I'm late.

Happy I just got here. Uh, Miss—?

Girl Forsythe.

Happy Miss Forsythe, this is my brother.

Biff Is Dad here?

Happy His name is Biff. You might've heard of him. Great football player.

Girl Really? What team?

Happy Are you familiar with football?

Girl No, I'm afraid I'm not.

Happy Bill is quarterback with the New York Giants.

Girl Well, that is nice, isn't it? (*She drinks.*)

Happy Good health.

Girl I'm happy to meet you.

Happy That's my name. Hap. It's really Harold, but at West Point they called me Happy.

Girl (*now really impressed*) Oh, I see. How do you do? (*She turns her profile.*)

Biff Isn't Dad coming?

Happy You want her?

Biff Oh, I could never make that.

Happy I remember the time that idea would never come into your head. Where's the old confidence, Biff?

Biff I just saw Oliver—

Happy Wait a minute. I've got to see that old confidence again. Do you want her? She's on call.

Biff Oh, no. (*He turns to look at the* **Girl**.)

Happy I'm telling you. (*Watch this. Turning to the* **Girl**:) Honey? (*She turns to him.*) Are you busy?

Girl Well, I am . . . but I could make a phone call.

Happy Do that, will you, honey? And see if you can get a friend. We'll be here for a while. Biff is one of the greatest football players in the country.

Girl (*standing up*) Well, I'm certainly happy to meet you.

Happy Come back soon.

Girl I'll try.

Happy Don't try, honey, try hard.

The **Girl** *exits.* **Stanley** *follows, shaking his head in bewildered admiration.*

Happy Isn't that a shame now? A beautiful girl like that? That's why I can't get married. There's not a good woman in a thousand. New York is loaded with them, kid!

Biff Hap, look—

Happy I told you she was on call!

Biff (*strangely unnerved*) Cut it out, will ya? I want to say something to you.

Happy Did you see Oliver?

Biff I saw him all right. Now look, I want to tell Dad a couple of things and I want you to help me.

Happy What? Is he going to back you?

Biff Are you crazy? You're out of your goddam head, you know that?

Happy Why? What happened?

Biff (*breathlessly*) I did a terrible thing today, Hap. It's been the strangest day I ever went through. I'm all numb, I swear.

Happy You mean he wouldn't see you?

Biff Well, I waited six hours for him, see? All day. Kept sending my name in. Even tried to date his secretary so she'd get me to him, but no soap.

Happy Because you're not showin' the old confidence, Biff. He remembered you, didn't he?

Biff (*stopping* **Happy** *with a gesture*) Finally, about five o'clock, he comes out. Didn't remember who I was or anything. I felt like such an idiot, Hap.

Happy Did you tell him my Florida idea?

Biff He walked away. I saw him for one minute. I got so mad I could've torn the walls down! How the hell did I ever get the idea I was a salesman there? I even believed myself that I'd been a salesman for him! And then he gave me one look and—I realized what a ridiculous lie my whole life has been! We've been talking in a dream for fifteen years. I was a shipping clerk.

Happy What'd you do?

Biff (*with great tension and wonder*) Well, he left, see. And the secretary went out. I was all alone in the waiting-room. I don't know what came over me, Hap. The next thing I know I'm in his office—paneled walls, everything. I can't explain it. I—Hap, I took his fountain pen.

Happy Geez, did he catch you?

Biff I ran out. I ran down all eleven flights. I ran and ran and ran.

Happy That was an awful dumb—what'd you do that for?

Biff (*agonized*) I don't know, I just—wanted to take something, I don't know. You gotta help me, Hap, I'm gonna tell Pop.

Happy You crazy? What for?

Biff Hap, he's got to understand that I'm not the man somebody lends that kind of money to. He thinks I've been spiting him all these years and it's eating him up.

Happy That's just it. You tell him something nice.

Biff I can't.

Happy Say you got a lunch date with Oliver tomorrow.

Biff So what do I do tomorrow?

Happy You leave the house tomorrow and come back at night and say Oliver is thinking it over. And he thinks it over for a couple of weeks, and gradually it fades away and nobody's the worse.

Biff But it'll go on forever!

Happy Dad is never so happy as when he's looking forward to something!

Willy *enters.*

Happy Hello, scout!

Willy Gee, I haven't been here in years!

Stanley *has followed* **Willy** *in and sets a chair for him.* **Stanley** *starts off but* **Happy** *stops him.*

Happy Stanley!

Stanley *stands by, waiting for an order.*

Biff (*going to* **Willy** *with guilt, as to an invalid*) Sit down, Pop. You want a drink?

Willy Sure, I don't mind.

Biff Let's get a load on.

Willy You look worried.

Biff N-no. (*To* **Stanley**:) Scotch all around. Make it doubles.

Stanley Doubles, right. (*He goes.*)

Willy You had a couple already, didn't you?

Biff Just a couple, yeah.

Willy Well, what happened, boy? (*Nodding affirmatively, with a smile:*) Everything go all right?

Biff (*takes a breath, then reaches out and grasps* **Willy***'s hand*) Pal . . . (*He is smiling bravely, and* **Willy** *is smiling too.*) I had an experience today.

Happy Terrific, Pop.

Willy That so? What happened?

Biff (*high, slightly alcoholic, above the earth*) I'm going to tell you everything from first to last. It's been a strange day. (*Silence. He looks around, composes himself as best he can, but his breath keeps breaking the rhythm of his voice.*) I had to wait quite a while for him, and—

Willy Oliver?

Biff Yeah, Oliver. All day, as a matter of cold fact. And a lot of—instances—facts, Pop, facts about my life came back to me. Who was it, Pop? Who ever said I was a salesman with Oliver?

Willy Well, you were.

Biff No, Dad, I was a shipping clerk.

Willy But you were practically—

Biff (*with determination*) Dad, I don't know who said it first, but I was never a salesman for Bill Oliver.

Willy What're you talking about?

Biff Let's hold on to the facts tonight, Pop. We're not going to get anywhere bullin' around. I was a shipping clerk.

Willy (*angrily*) All right, now listen to me—

Biff Why don't you let me finish?

Willy I'm not interested in stories about the past or any crap of that kind because the woods are burning, boys, you understand? There's a big blaze going on all around. I was fired today.

Biff (*shocked*) How could you be?

Willy I was fired, and I'm looking for a little good news to tell your mother, because the woman has waited and the woman has suffered. The gist of it is that I haven't got a story left in my head, Biff. So don't give me a lecture about facts and aspects. I am not interested. Now what've you got to say to me?

Stanley *enters with three drinks. They wait until he leaves.*

Willy Did you see Oliver?

Biff Jesus, Dad!

Willy You mean you didn't go up there?

Happy Sure he went up there.

Biff I did. I—saw him. How could they fire you?

Willy (*on the edge of his chair*) What kind of a welcome did he give you?

Biff He won't even let you work on commission?

Willy I'm out! (*Driving:*) So tell me, he gave you a warm welcome?

Happy Sure, Pop, sure!

Biff (*driven*) Well, it was kind of—

Willy I was wondering if he'd remember you. (*To* **Happy**:) Imagine, man doesn't see him for ten, twelve years and gives him that kind of a welcome!

Happy Damn right!

Biff (*trying to return to the offensive*) Pop, look—

Willy You know why he remembered you, don't you? Because you impressed him in those days.

Biff Let's talk quietly and get this down to the facts, huh?

Willy (*as though* **Biff** *had been interrupting*) Well, what happened? It's great news, Biff. Did he take you into his office or'd you talk in the waiting-room?

Biff Well, he came in, see, and—

Willy (*with a big smile*) What'd he say? Betcha he threw his arm around you.

Biff Well, he kinda—

Willy He's a fine man. (*To* **Happy**:) Very hard man to see, y'know.

Happy (*agreeing*) Oh, I know.

Willy (*to* **Biff**) Is that where you had the drinks?

Biff Yeah, he gave me a couple of—no, no!

Happy (*cutting in*) He told him my Florida idea.

Willy Don't interrupt. (*To* **Biff**:) How'd he react to the Florida idea?

Biff Dad, will you give me a minute to explain?

Willy I've been waiting for you to explain since I sat down here! What happened? He took you into his office and what?

Biff Well—I talked. And—and he listened, see.

Willy Famous for the way he listens, y'know. What was his answer?

Biff His answer was—(*He breaks off, suddenly angry.*) Dad, you're not letting me tell you what I want to tell you!

Willy (*accusing, angered*) You didn't see him, did you?

Biff I did see him!

Willy What'd you insult him or something? You insulted him, didn't you?

Biff Listen, will you let me out of it, will you just let me out of it!

Happy What the hell!

Willy Tell me what happened!

Biff (*to* **Happy**) I can't talk to him!

A single trumpet note jars the ear. The light of green leaves stains the house, which holds the air of night and a dream. **Young Bernard** *enters and knocks on the door of the house.*

Young Bernard (*frantically*) Mrs. Loman, Mrs. Loman!

Happy Tell him what happened!

Biff (*to* **Happy**) Shut up and leave me alone!

Willy No, no! You had to go and flunk math!

Biff What math? What're you talking about?

Young Bernard Mrs. Loman, Mrs. Loman!

Linda *appears in the house, as of old.*

Willy (*wildly*) Math, math, math!

Biff Take it easy, Pop!

Young Bernard Mrs. Loman!

Willy (*furiously*) If you hadn't flunked you'd've been set by now!

Biff Now, look, I'm gonna tell you what happened, and you're going to listen to me.

Young Bernard Mrs. Loman!

Biff I waited six hours—

Happy What the hell are you saying?

Biff I kept sending in my name but he wouldn't see me. So finally he . . . (*He continues unheard as light fades low on the restaurant.*)

Young Bernard Biff flunked math!

Linda No!

Young Bernard Birnbaum flunked him! They won't graduate him!

Linda But they have to. He's gotta go to the university. Where is he? Biff! Biff!

Young Bernard No, he left. He went to Grand Central.

Linda Grand—You mean he went to Boston!

Young Bernard Is Uncle Willy in Boston?

Linda Oh, maybe Willy can talk to the teacher. Oh, the poor, poor boy!

Light on house area snaps out.

Biff (*at the table, now audible, holding up a gold fountain pen*) . . . so I'm washed up with Oliver, you understand? Are you listening to me?

Willy (*at a loss*) Yeah, sure. If you hadn't flunked—

Biff Flunked what? What're you talking about?

Willy Don't blame everything on me! I didn't flunk math—you did! What pen?

Happy That was awful dumb, Biff, a pen like that is worth—

Willy (*seeing the pen for the first time*) You took Oliver's pen?

Biff (*weakening*) Dad, I just explained it to you.

Willy You stole Bill Oliver's fountain pen!

Biff I didn't exactly steal it! That's just what I've been explaining to you!

Happy He had it in his hand and just then Oliver walked in, so he got nervous and stuck it in his pocket!

Willy My God, Biff!

Biff I never intended to do it, Dad!

Operator's Voice Standish Arms, good evening!

Willy (*shouting*) I'm not in my room!

Biff (*frightened*) Dad, what's the matter? (*He and* **Happy** *stand up.*)

Operator Ringing Mr. Loman for you!

Willy I'm not there, stop it!

Biff (*horrified, gets down on one knee before* **Willy**) Dad, I'll make good, I'll make good. (**Willy** *tries to get to his feet.* **Biff** *holds him down.*) Sit down now.

Willy No, you're no good, you're no good for anything.

Biff I am, Dad, I'll find something else, you understand? Now don't worry about anything. (*He holds up* **Willy***'s face:*) Talk to me, Dad.

Operator Mr. Loman does not answer. Shall I page him?

Willy (*attempting to stand, as though to rush and silence the* **Operator**) No, no, no!

Happy He'll strike something, Pop.

Willy No, no . . .

Biff (*desperately, standing over* **Willy**) Pop, listen! Listen to me! I'm telling you something good. Oliver talked to his partner about the Florida idea. You listening? He—he talked to his partner, and he came to me . . . I'm going to be all right, you hear? Dad, listen to me, he said it was just a question of the amount!

Willy Then you . . . got it?

Happy He's gonna be terrific, Pop!

Willy (*trying to stand*) Then you got it, haven't you? You got it! You got it!

Biff (*agonized, holds* **Willy** *down*) No, no. Look, Pop. I'm supposed to have lunch with them tomorrow. I'm just telling you this so you'll know that I can still make an impression, Pop. And I'll make good somewhere, but I can't go tomorrow, see?

Willy Why not? You simply—

Biff But the pen, Pop!

Willy You give it to him and tell him it was an oversight!

Happy Sure, have lunch tomorrow!

Biff I can't say that—

Willy You were doing a crossword puzzle and accidentally used his pen!

Biff Listen, kid, I took those balls years ago, now I walk in with his fountain pen? That clinches it, don't you see? I can't face him like that! I'll try elsewhere.

Page's Voice Paging Mr. Loman!

Willy Don't you want to be anything?

Biff Pop, how can I go back?

Willy You don't want to be anything, is that what's behind it?

Biff (*now angry at* **Willy** *for not crediting his sympathy*) Don't take it that way! You think it was easy walking into that office after what I'd done to him? A team of horses couldn't have dragged me back to Bill Oliver!

Willy Then why'd you go?

Biff Why did I go? Why did I go! Look at you! Look at what's become of you!

Off left, **The Woman** *laughs.*

Willy Biff, you're going to go to that lunch tomorrow, or—

Biff I can't go. I've got no appointment!

Happy Biff, for . . .!

Willy Are you spiting me?

Biff Don't take it that way! Goddammit!

Willy (*strikes* **Biff** *and falters away from the table*) You rotten little louse! Are you spiting me?

The Woman Someone's at the door, Willy!

Biff I'm no good, can't you see what I am?

Happy (*separating them*) Hey, you're in a restaurant! Now cut it out, both of you? (*The girls enter.*) Hello, girls, sit down.

The Woman *laughs, off left.*

Miss Forsythe I guess we might as well. This is Letta.

The Woman Willy, are you going to wake up?

Biff (*ignoring* **Willy**) How're ya, miss, sit down. What do you drink?

Miss Forsythe Letta might not be able to stay long.

Letta I gotta get up very early tomorrow. I got jury duty. I'm so excited! Were you fellows ever on a jury?

Biff No, but I been in front of them! (*The girls laugh.*) This is my father.

Letta Isn't he cute? Sit down with us, Pop.

Happy Sit him down, Biff!

Biff (*going to him*) Come on, slugger, drink us under the table. To hell with it! Come on, sit down, pal.

On **Biff***'s last insistence,* **Willy** *is about to sit.*

The Woman (*now urgently*) Willy, are you going to answer the door!

The Woman*'s call pulls* **Willy** *back. He starts right, befuddled.*

Biff Hey, where are you going?

Willy Open the door.

Biff The door?

Willy The washroom . . . the door . . . where's the door?

Biff (*leading* **Willy** *to the left*) Just go straight down.

Willy *moves left.*

The Woman Willy, Willy, are you going to get up, get up, get up, get up?

Willy *exits left.*

Letta I think it's sweet you bring your daddy along.

Miss Forsythe Oh, he isn't really your father!

Biff (*at left, turning to her resentfully*) Miss Forsythe, you've just seen a prince walk by. A fine, troubled prince. A hardworking, unappreciated prince. A pal, you understand? A good companion. Always for his boys.

Letta That's so sweet.

Happy Well, girls, what's the program? We're wasting time. Come on, Biff. Gather round. Where would you like to go?

Biff Why don't you do something for him?

Happy Me!

Biff Don't you give a damn for him, Hap?

Happy What're you talking about? I'm the one who—

Biff I sense it, you don't give a good goddam about him. (*He takes the rolled-up hose from his pocket and puts it on the table in* *front of* **Happy**.) Look what I found in the cellar, for Christ's sake. How can you bear to let it go on?

Happy Me? Who goes away? Who runs off and—

Biff Yeah, but he doesn't mean anything to you. You could help him—I can't! Don't you understand what I'm talking about? He's going to kill himself, don't you know that?

Happy Don't I know it! Me!

Biff Hap, help him! Jesus . . . help him . . . Help me, help me, I can't bear to look at his face! (*Ready to weep, he hurries out, up right.*)

Happy (*starting after him*) Where are you going?

Miss Forsythe What's he so mad about?

Happy Come on, girls, we'll catch up with him.

Miss Forsythe (*as* **Happy** *pushes her out*) Say, I don't like that temper of his!

Happy He's just a little overstrung, he'll be all right!

Willy (*off left, as* **The Woman** *laughs*) Don't answer! Don't answer!

Letta Don't you want to tell your father—

Happy No, that's not my father. He's just a guy. Come on, we'll catch Biff, and, honey, we're going to paint this town! Stanley, where's the check! Hey, Stanley!

They exit. **Stanley** *looks toward left.*

Stanley (*calling to* **Happy** *indignantly*) Mr. Loman! Mr. Loman!

Stanley *picks up a chair and follows them off. Knocking is heard off left.* **The Woman** *enters, laughing.* **Willy** *follows her. She is in a black slip; he is buttoning his shirt. Raw, sensuous music accompanies their speech.*

Willy Will you stop laughing? Will you stop?

The Woman Aren't you going to answer the door? He'll wake the whole hotel.

Willy I'm not expecting anybody.

The Woman Whyn't you have another drink, honey, and stop being so damn self-centered?

Willy I'm so lonely.

The Woman You know you ruined me, Willy? From now on, whenever you come to the office, I'll see that you go right through to the buyers. No waiting at my desk any more, Willy. You ruined me.

Willy That's nice of you to say that.

The Woman Gee, you are self-centered! Why so sad? You are the saddest, self-centeredest soul I ever did see-saw. (*She laughs. He kisses her.*) Come on inside, drummer boy. It's silly to be dressing in the middle of the night. (*As knocking is heard:*) Aren't you going to answer the door?

Willy They're knocking on the wrong door.

The Woman But I felt the knocking. And he heard us talking in here. Maybe the hotel's on fire!

Willy (*his terror rising*) It's a mistake.

The Woman Then tell him to go away!

Willy There's nobody there.

The Woman It's getting on my nerves, Willy. There's somebody standing out there and it's getting on my nerves!

Willy (*pushing her away from him*) All right, stay in the bathroom here, and don't come out. I think there's a law in Massachusetts about it, so don't come out. It may be that new room clerk. He looked very mean. So don't come out. It's a mistake, there's no fire.

The knocking is heard again. He takes a few steps away from her, and she vanishes into the wing. The light follows him, and now he is facing **Young Biff**, *who carries a suitcase.* **Biff** *steps toward him. The music is gone.*

Biff Why didn't you answer?

Willy Biff! What are you doing in Boston?

Biff Why didn't you answer? I've been knocking for five minutes, I called you on the phone—

Willy I just heard you. I was in the bathroom and had the door shut. Did anything happen home?

Biff Dad—I let you down.

Willy What do you mean?

Biff Dad . . .

Willy Biffo, what's this about? (*Putting his arm around* **Biff**:) Come on, let's go downstairs and get you a malted.

Biff Dad, I flunked math.

Willy Not for the term?

Biff The term. I haven't got enough credits to graduate.

Willy You mean to say Bernard wouldn't give you the answers?

Biff He did, he tried, but I only got a sixty-one.

Willy And they wouldn't give you four points?

Biff Birnbaum refused absolutely. I begged him, Pop, but he won't give me those points. You gotta talk to him before they close the school. Because if he saw the kind of man you are, and you just talked to him in your way, I'm sure he'd come through for me. The class came right before practice, see, and I didn't go enough. Would you talk to him? He'd like you, Pop. You know the way you could talk.

Willy You're on. We'll drive right back.

Biff Oh, Dad, good work! I'm sure he'll change it for you!

Willy Go downstairs and tell the clerk I'm checkin' out. Go right down.

Biff Yes, sir! See, the reason he hates me, Pop—one day he was late for class so I got up at the blackboard and imitated him. I crossed my eyes and talked with a lithp.

Willy (*laughing*) You did? The kids like it?

Biff They nearly died laughing!

Willy Yeah? What'd you do?

Biff The thquare root of thixthy twee is . . . (**Willy** *bursts out laughing;* **Biff** *joins him.*) And in the middle of it he walked in!

Willy *laughs and* **The Woman** *joins in offstage.*

Willy (*without hesitation*) Hurry downstairs and—

Biff Somebody in there?

Willy No, that was next door.

The Woman *laughs offstage.*

Biff Somebody got in your bathroom!

Willy No, it's the next room, there's a party—

The Woman (*enters, laughing. She lisps this*) Can I come in? There's something in the bathtub, Willy, and it's moving!

Willy *looks at* **Biff***, who is staring open-mouthed and horrified at* **The Woman**.

Willy Ah—you better go back to your room. They must be finished painting by now. They're painting her room so I let her take a shower here. Go back, go back . . . (*He pushes her.*)

The Woman (*resisting*) But I've got to get dressed, Willy, I can't—

Willy Get out of here! Go back, go back . . . (*Suddenly striving for the ordinary:*) This is Miss Francis, Biff, she's a buyer. They're painting her room. Go back, Miss Francis, go back . . .

The Woman But my clothes, I can't go out naked in the hall!

Willy (*pushing her offstage*) Get outa here! Go back, go back!

Biff *slowly sits down on his suitcase as the argument continues offstage.*

The Woman Where's my stockings? You promised me stockings, Willy!

Willy I have no stockings here!

The Woman You had two boxes of size nine sheers for me, and I want them!

Willy Here, for God's sake, will you get outa here!

The Woman (*enters holding a box of stockings*) I just hope there's nobody in the hall. That's all I—hope. (*To* **Biff**:) Are you football or baseball?

Biff Football.

The Woman (*angry, humiliated*) That's me too. G'night. (*She snatches her clothes from* **Willy**, *and walks out.*)

Willy (*after a pause*) Well, better get going. I want to get to the school first thing in the morning. Get my suits out of the closet. I'll get my valise. (**Biff** *doesn't move.*) What's the matter? (**Biff** *remains motionless, tears falling.*) She's a buyer. Buys for J. H. Simmons. She lives down the hall—they're painting. You don't imagine—(*He breaks off. After a pause:*) Now listen, pal, she's just a buyer. She sees merchandise in her room and they have to keep it looking just so . . . (*Pause. Assuming command:*) All right, get my suits. (**Biff** *doesn't move.*) Now stop crying and do as I say. I gave you an order. Biff, I gave you an order! Is that what you do when I give you an order? How dare you cry! (*Putting his arm around* **Biff**:) Now look, Biff, when you grow up you'll understand about these things. You mustn't—you mustn't overemphasize a thing like this. I'll see Birnbaum first thing in the morning.

Biff Never mind.

Willy (*getting down beside* **Biff**) Never mind! He's going to give you those points. I'll see to it.

Biff He wouldn't listen to you.

Willy He certainly will listen to me. You need those points for the U. of Virginia.

Biff I'm not going there.

Willy Heh? If I can't get him to change that mark you'll make it up in summer school. You've got all summer to—

Biff (*his weeping breaking from him*) Dad . . .

Willy (*infected by it*) Oh, my boy . . .

Biff Dad . . .

Willy She's nothing to me, Biff. I was lonely, I was terribly lonely.

Biff You—you gave her Mama's stockings! (*His tears break through and he rises to go.*)

Willy (*grabbing for* **Biff**) I gave you an order!

Biff Don't touch me, you—liar!

Willy Apologize for that!

Biff You fake! You phony little fake! You fake! (*Overcome, he turns quickly and weeping fully goes out with his suitcase.* **Willy** *is left on the floor on his knees.*)

Willy I gave you an order! Biff, come back here or I'll beat you! Come back here! I'll whip you!

Stanley *comes quickly in from the right and stands in front of* **Willy**.

Willy (*shouts at* **Stanley**) I gave you an order . . .

Stanley Hey, let's pick it up, pick it up, Mr. Loman. (*He helps* **Willy** *to his feet.*) Your boys left with the chippies. They said they'll see you home.

A second **Waiter** *watches some distance away.*

Willy But we were supposed to have dinner together.

Music is heard, **Willy***'s theme.*

Stanley Can you make it?

Willy I'll—sure, I can make it. (*Suddenly concerned about his clothes:*) Do I—I look all right?

Stanley Sure, you look all right. (*He flicks a speck off* **Willy***'s lapel.*)

Willy Here—here's a dollar.

Stanley Oh, your son paid me. It's all right.

Willy (*putting it in* **Stanley***'s hand*) No, take it. You're a good boy.

Stanley Oh, no, you don't have to . . .

Willy Here—here's some more, I don't need it any more. (*After a slight pause:*) Tell me—is there a seed store in the neighborhood?

Stanley Seeds? You mean like to plant?

As **Willy** *turns,* **Stanley** *slips the money back into his jacket pocket.*

Willy Yes. Carrots, peas . . .

Stanley Well, there's hardware stores on Sixth Avenue, but it may be too late now.

Willy (*anxiously*) Oh, I'd better hurry. I've got to get some seeds. (*He starts off to the right.*) I've got to get some seeds, right away. Nothing's planted. I don't have a thing in the ground.

Willy *hurries out as the light goes down.* **Stanley** *moves over to the right after him, watches him off. The other* **Waiter** *has been staring at* **Willy**.

Stanley (*to the* **Waiter**) Well, whatta you looking at?

The **Waiter** *picks up the chairs and moves off right.* **Stanley** *takes the table and follows him. The light fades on this area. There is a long pause, the sound of the flute coming over. The light gradually rises on the kitchen, which is empty.* **Happy** *appears at the door of* *the house, followed by* **Biff**. **Happy** *is carrying a large bunch of long-stemmed roses. He enters the kitchen, looks around for* **Linda**. *Not seeing her, he turns to* **Biff**, *who is just outside the house door, and makes a gesture with his hands, indicating "Not here, I guess." He looks into the living-room and freezes. Inside,* **Linda**, *unseen, is seated,* **Willy***'s coat on her lap. She rises ominously and quietly and moves toward* **Happy**, *who backs up into the kitchen, afraid.*

Happy Hey, what're you doing up? (**Linda** *says nothing but moves toward him implacably.*) Where's Pop? (*He keeps backing to the right, and now* **Linda** *is in full view in the doorway to the living-room.*) Is he sleeping?

Linda Where were you?

Happy (*trying to laugh it off*) We met two girls, Mom, very fine types. Here, we brought you some flowers. (*Offering them to her:*) Put them in your room, Ma.

She knocks them to the floor at **Biff***'s feet. He has now come inside and closed the door behind him. She stares at* **Biff**, *silent.*

Happy Now what'd you do that for? Mom, I want you to have some flowers—

Linda (*cutting* **Happy** *off, violently to* **Biff**) Don't you care whether he lives or dies?

Happy (*going to the stairs*) Come upstairs, Biff.

Biff (*with a flare of disgust, to* **Happy**) Go away from me! (*To* **Linda**:) What do you mean, lives or dies? Nobody's dying around here, pal.

Linda Get out of my sight! Get out of here!

Biff I wanna see the boss.

Linda You're not going near him!

Biff Where is he? (*He moves into the living-room and* **Linda** *follows.*)

Linda (*shouting after* **Biff**) You invite him for dinner. He looks forward to it all day (**Biff** *appears in his parents' bedroom, looks around, and exits*) and then you desert him there. There's no stranger you'd do that to!

Happy Why? He had a swell time with us. Listen, when I (**Linda** *comes back into the kitchen*) desert him I hope I don't outlive the day!

Linda Get out of here!

Happy Now look, Mom . . .

Linda Did you have to go to women tonight? You and your lousy rotten whores!

Biff *re-enters the kitchen.*

Happy Mom, all we did was follow Biff around trying to cheer him up! (*To* **Biff**:) Boy, what a night you gave me!

Linda Get out of here, both of you, and don't come back! I don't want you tormenting him any more. Go on now, get your things together! (*To* **Biff**:) You can sleep in his apartment. (*She starts to pick up the flowers and stops herself.*) Pick up this stuff, I'm not your maid any more. Pick it up, you bum, you!

Happy *turns his back to her in refusal.* **Biff** *slowly moves over and gets down on his knees, picking up the flowers.*

Linda You're a pair of animals! Not one, not another living soul would have had the cruelty to walk out on that man in a restaurant!

Biff (*not looking at her*) Is that what he said?

Linda He didn't have to say anything. He was so humiliated he nearly limped when he came in.

Happy But, Mom, he had a great time with us—

Biff (*cutting him off violently*) Shut up!

Without another word, **Happy** *goes upstairs.*

Linda You! You didn't even go in to see if he was all right!

Biff (*still on the floor in front of* **Linda**, *the flowers in his hand; with self-loathing*) No. Didn't. Didn't do a damned thing. How do you like that, heh? Left him babbling in a toilet.

Linda You louse. You . . .

Biff Now you hit it on the nose! (*He gets up, throws the flowers in the wastebasket.*) The scum of the earth, and you're looking at him!

Linda Get out of here!

Biff I gotta talk to the boss, Mom. Where is he?

Linda You're not going near him. Get out of this house!

Biff (*with absolute assurance, determination*) No. We're gonna have an abrupt conversation, him and me.

Linda You're not talking to him!

Hammering is heard from outside the house, off right. **Biff** *turns toward the noise.*

Linda (*suddenly pleading*) Will you please leave him alone?

Biff What's he doing out there?

Linda He's planting the garden!

Biff (*quietly*) Now? Oh, my God!

Biff *moves outside,* **Linda** *following. The light dies down on them and comes up on the center of the apron as* **Willy** *walks into it. He is carrying a flashlight, a hoe, and a handful of seed packets. He raps the top of the hoe sharply to fix it firmly, and then moves to the left, measuring off the distance with his foot. He holds the flashlight to look at the seed packets, reading off the instructions. He is in the blue of night.*

Willy Carrots . . . quarter-inch apart. Rows . . . one-foot rows. (*He measures it off.*) One foot. (*He puts down a package and measures off.*) Beets. (*He puts down another package and measures again.*) Lettuce. (*He reads the package, puts it down.*) One foot—(*He breaks off as* **Ben** *appears at the right and moves slowly down to him.*) What a proposition, ts, ts. Terrific, terrific. 'Cause she's suffered, Ben, the woman has suffered. You understand me? A man can't go out the way he came in, Ben, a man has got to add up to something. You can't, you can't—(**Ben** *moves toward him as though to interrupt.*) You gotta consider, now. Don't answer so quick. Remember, it's a guaranteed twenty-thousand-dollar proposition. Now look, Ben, I want you to go through the ins and outs of this thing with me. I've got nobody to talk to, Ben, and the woman has suffered, you hear me?

Ben (*standing still, considering*) What's the proposition?

Willy It's twenty thousand dollars on the barrelhead. Guaranteed, gilt-edged, you understand?

Ben You don't want to make a fool of yourself. They might not honor the policy.

Willy How can they dare refuse? Didn't I work like a coolie to meet every premium on the nose? And now they don't pay off! Impossible!

Ben It's called a cowardly thing, William.

Willy Why? Does it take more guts to stand here the rest of my life ringing up a zero?

Ben (*yielding*) That's a point, William. (*He moves, thinking, turns.*) And twenty thousand—that *is* something one can feel with the hand, it is there.

Willy (*now assured, with rising power*) Oh, Ben, that's the whole beauty of it! I see it like a diamond, shining in the dark, hard and rough, that I can pick up and touch in my hand. Not like—like an appointment! This would not be another damned-fool appointment, Ben, and it changes all the aspects. Because he thinks I'm nothing, see, and so he spites me. But the funeral—(*Straightening up:*) Ben, that funeral will be massive! They'll come from Maine, Massachusetts, Vermont, New Hampshire! All the old-timers with the strange license plates—that boy will be thunder-struck, Ben, because he never realized—I am known! Rhode Island, New York, New Jersey—I am known, Ben, and he'll see it with his eyes once and for all. He'll see what I am, Ben! He's in for a shock, that boy!

Ben (*coming down to the edge of the garden*) He'll call you a coward.

Willy (*suddenly fearful*) No, that would be terrible.

Ben Yes. And a damned fool.

Willy No, no, he mustn't, I won't have that! (*He is broken and desperate.*)

Ben He'll hate you, William.

The gay music of the boys is heard.

Willy Oh, Ben, how do we get back to all the great times? Used to be so full of light, and comradeship, the sleigh-riding in winter, and the ruddiness on his cheeks. And always some kind of good news coming up, always something nice coming up ahead. And never even let me carry the valises in the house, and simonizing, simonizing that little red car! Why, why can't I give him something and not have him hate me?

Ben Let me think about it. (*He glances at his watch.*) I still have a little time. Remarkable proposition, but you've got to be sure you're not making a fool of yourself.

Ben *drifts off upstage and goes out of sight.* **Biff** *comes down from the left.*

Willy (*suddenly conscious of* **Biff**, *turns and looks up at him, then begins picking up the packages of seeds in confusion*) Where the hell is that seed? (*Indignantly:*) You can't see nothing out here! They boxed in the whole goddam neighborhood!

Biff There are people all around here. Don't you realize that?

Willy I'm busy. Don't bother me.

Biff (*taking the hoe from* **Willy**) I'm saying good-by to you, Pop. (**Willy** *looks at him, silent, unable to move.*) I'm not coming back any more.

Willy You're not going to see Oliver tomorrow?

Biff I've got no appointment, Dad.

Willy He put his arm around you, and you've got no appointment?

Biff Pop, get this now, will you? Everytime I've left it's been a fight that sent me out of here. Today I realized something about myself and I tried to explain it to you and I—I think I'm just not smart enough to make any sense out of it for you. To hell with whose fault it is or anything like that. (*He takes* **Willy***'s arm.*) Let's just wrap it up, heh? Come on in, we'll tell Mom. (*He gently tries to pull* **Willy** *to left.*)

Willy (*frozen, immobile, with guilt in his voice*) No, I don't want to see her.

Biff Come on! (*He pulls again, and* **Willy** *tries to pull away.*)

Willy (*highly nervous*) No, no, I don't want to see her.

Biff (*tries to look into* **Willy***'s face, as if to find the answer there*) Why don't you want to see her?

Willy (*more harshly now*) Don't bother me, will you?

Biff What do you mean, you don't want to see her? You don't want them calling you yellow, do you? This isn't your fault; it's me, I'm a bum. Now come inside! (**Willy** *strains to get away.*) Did you hear what I said to you?

Willy *pulls away and quickly goes by himself into the house.* **Biff** *follows.*

Linda (*to* **Willy**) Did you plant, dear?

Biff (*at the door, to* **Linda**) All right, we had it out. I'm going and I'm not writing any more.

Linda (*going to* **Willy** *in the kitchen*) I think that's the best way, dear. 'Cause there's no use drawing it out, you'll just never get along.

Willy *doesn't respond.*

Biff People ask where I am and what I'm doing, you don't know, and you don't care. That way it'll be off your mind and you can start brightening up again. All right? That clears it, doesn't it? (**Willy** *is silent, and* **Biff** *goes to him.*) You gonna wish me luck, scout? (*He extends his hand.*) What do you say?

Linda Shake his hand, Willy.

Willy (*turning to her, seething with hurt*) There's no necessity to mention the pen at all, y'know.

Biff (*gently*) I've got no appointment, Dad.

Willy (*erupting fiercely*) He put his arm around . . .?

Biff Dad, you're never going to see what I am, so what's the use of arguing? If I strike oil I'll send you a check. Meantime forget I'm alive.

Willy (*to* **Linda**) Spite, see?

Biff Shake hands, Dad.

Willy Not my hand.

Biff I was hoping not to go this way.

Willy Well, this is the way you're going. Good-by.

Biff *looks at him a moment, then turns sharply and goes to the stairs.*

Willy (*stops him with*) May you rot in hell if you leave this house!

Biff (*turning*) Exactly what is it that you want from me?

Willy I want you to know, on the train, in the mountains, in the valleys, wherever you go, that you cut down your life for spite!

Biff No, no.

Willy Spite, spite, is the word of your undoing! And when you're down and out, remember what did it. When you're rotting somewhere beside the railroad tracks, remember, and don't you dare blame it on me!

Biff I'm not blaming it on you!

Willy I won't take the rap for this, you hear?

Happy *comes down the stairs and stands on the bottom step, watching.*

Biff That's just what I'm telling you!

Willy (*sinking into a chair at the table, with full accusation*) You're trying to put a knife in me—don't think I don't know what you're doing!

Biff All right, phony! Then let's lay it on the line. (*He whips the rubber tube out of his pocket and puts it on the table.*)

Happy You crazy—

Linda Biff! (*She moves to grab the hose, but* **Biff** *holds it down with his hand.*)

Biff Leave it there! Don't move it!

Willy (*not looking at it*) What is that?

Biff You know goddam well what that is.

Willy (*caged, wanting to escape*) I never saw that.

Biff You saw it. The mice didn't bring it into the cellar! What is this supposed to do, make a hero out of you? This supposed to make me sorry for you?

Willy Never heard of it.

Biff There'll be no pity for you, you hear it? No pity!

Willy (*to* **Linda**) You hear the spite!

Biff No, you're going to hear the truth—what you are and what I am!

Linda Stop it!

Willy Spite!

Happy (*coming down toward* **Biff**) You cut it now!

Biff (*to* **Happy**) The man don't know who we are! The man is gonna know! (*To* **Willy**:) We never told the truth for ten minutes in this house!

Happy We always told the truth!

Biff (*turning on him*) You big blow, are you the assistant buyer? You're one of the two assistants to the assistant, aren't you?

Happy Well, I'm practically—

Biff You're practically full of it! We all are! And I'm through with it. (*To* **Willy**:) Now hear this, Willy, this is me.

Willy I know you!

Biff You know why I had no address for three months? I stole a suit in Kansas City and I was in jail. (*To* **Linda**, *who is sobbing:*) Stop crying. I'm through with it.

Linda *turns away from them, her hands covering her face.*

Willy I suppose that's my fault!

Biff I stole myself out of every good job since high school!

Willy And whose fault is that?

Biff And I never got anywhere because you blew me so full of hot air I could never stand taking orders from anybody! That's whose fault it is!

Willy I hear that!

Linda Don't, Biff!

Biff It's goddam time you heard that! I had to be boss big shot in two weeks, and I'm through with it!

Willy Then hang yourself! For spite, hang yourself!

Biff No! Nobody's hanging himself, Willy! I ran down eleven flights with a pen in my hand today. And suddenly I stopped, you hear me? And in the middle of that office building, do you hear this? I stopped in the middle of that building and I saw—the sky. I saw the things that I love in this world. The work and the food and time to sit and smoke. And I looked at the pen and said to myself, what the hell am I grabbing this for? Why am I trying to become what I don't want to be? What am I doing in an office, making a contemptuous, begging fool of myself, when all I want is out there, waiting for me the minute I say I know who I am! Why can't I say that, Willy? (*He tries to make* **Willy** *face him, but* **Willy** *pulls away and moves to the left.*)

Willy (*with hatred, threateningly*) The door of your life is wide open!

Biff Pop! I'm a dime a dozen, and so are you!

Willy (*turning on him now in an uncontrolled outburst*) I am not a dime a dozen! I am Willy Loman, and you are Biff Loman!

Biff *starts for* **Willy**, *but is blocked by* **Happy**. *In his fury,* **Biff** *seems on the verge of attacking his father.*

Biff I am not a leader of men, Willy, and neither are you. You were never anything but a hard-working drummer who landed in the ash can like all the rest of them! I'm one dollar an hour, Willy! I tried seven states and couldn't raise it. A buck an hour! Do you gather my meaning? I'm not bringing home any prizes any more, and you're going to stop waiting for me to bring them home!

Willy (*directly to* **Biff**) You vengeful, spiteful mut!

Biff *breaks from* **Happy**. **Willy**, *in fright, starts up the stairs.* **Biff** *grabs him.*

Biff (*at the peak of his fury*) Pop, I'm nothing! I'm nothing, Pop. Can't you understand that? There's no spite in it any more. I'm just what I am, that's all.

Biff'*s fury has spent itself, and he breaks down, sobbing, holding on to* **Willy**, *who dumbly fumbles for* **Biff**'*s face.*

Willy (*astonished*) What're you doing? What're you doing? (*To* **Linda**.) Why is he crying?

Biff (*crying, broken*) Will you let me go, for Christ's sake? Will you take that phony dream and burn it before something happens?

(*Struggling to contain himself, he pulls away and moves to the stairs.*) I'll go in the morning. Put him—put him to bed. (*Exhausted,* **Biff** *moves up the stairs to his room.*)

Willy (*after a long pause, astonished, elevated*) Isn't that—isn't that remarkable? Biff—he likes me!

Linda He loves you, Willy!

Happy (*deeply moved*) Always did, Pop.

Willy Oh, Biff! (*Staring wildly:*) He cried! Cried to me. (*He is choking with his love, and now cries out his promise:*) That boy—that boy is going to be magnificent!

Ben *appears in the light just outside the kitchen.*

Ben Yes, outstanding, with twenty thousand behind him.

Linda (*sensing the racing of his mind, fearfully, carefully*) Now come to bed, Willy. It's all settled now.

Willy (*finding it difficult not to rush out of the house*) Yes, we'll sleep. Come on. Go to sleep, Hap.

Ben And it does take a great kind of a man to crack the jungle.

In accents of dread, **Ben***'s idyllic music starts up.*

Happy (*his arm around* **Linda**) I'm getting married, Pop, don't forget it. I'm changing everything. I'm gonna run that department before the year is up. You'll see, Mom. (*He kisses her.*)

Ben The jungle is dark but full of diamonds, Willy.

Willy *turns, moves, listening to* **Ben**.

Linda Be good. You're both good boys, just act that way, that's all.

Happy 'Night, Pop. (*He goes upstairs.*)

Linda (*to* **Willy**) Come, dear.

Ben (*with greater force*) One must go in to fetch a diamond out.

Willy (*to* **Linda***, as he moves slowly along the edge of the kitchen, toward the door*) I just want to get settled down, Linda. Let me sit alone for a little.

Linda (*almost uttering her fear*) I want you upstairs.

Willy (*taking her in his arms*) In a few minutes, Linda. I couldn't sleep right now. Go on, you look awful tired. (*He kisses her.*)

Ben Not like an appointment at all. A diamond is rough and hard to the touch.

Willy Go on now. I'll be right up.

Linda I think this is the only way, Willy.

Willy Sure, it's the best thing.

Ben Best thing!

Willy The only way. Everything is gonna be—go on, kid, get to bed. You look so tired.

Linda Come right up.

Willy Two minutes.

Linda *goes into the living-room, then reappears in her bedroom.* **Willy** *moves just outside the kitchen door.*

Willy Loves me. (*Wonderingly:*) Always loved me. Isn't that a remarkable thing? Ben, he'll worship me for it!

Ben (*with promise*) It's dark there, but full of diamonds.

Willy Can you imagine that magnificence with twenty thousand dollars in his pocket?

Linda (*calling from her room*) Willy! Come up!

Willy (*calling into the kitchen*) Yes! Yes. Coming! It's very smart, you realize that, don't you, sweetheart? Even Ben sees it. I gotta go, baby. 'By! 'By! (*Going over to* **Ben***, almost dancing:*) Imagine? When the mail comes he'll be ahead of Bernard again!

Ben A perfect proposition all around.

Willy Did you see how he cried to me? Oh, if I could kiss him, Ben!

Ben Time, William, time!

Willy Oh, Ben, I always knew one way or another we were gonna make it, Biff and I!

Ben (*looking at his watch*) The boat. We'll be late. (*He moves slowly off into the darkness.*)

Willy (*elegiacally, turning to the house*) Now when you kick off, boy, I want a seventy-yard boot, and get right down the field under the ball, and when you hit, hit low and hit hard, because it's important, boy. (*He swings around and faces the audience.*) There's all kinds of important people in the stands, and the first thing you know . . . (*Suddenly realizing he is alone:*) Ben! Ben, where do I . . .? (*He makes a sudden movement of search.*) Ben, how do I . . .?

Linda (*calling*) Willy, you coming up?

Willy (*uttering a gasp of fear, whirling about as if to quiet her*) Sh! (*He turns around as if to find his way; sounds, faces, voices, seem to be swarming in upon him and he flicks at them, crying,*) Sh! Sh! (*Suddenly music, faint and high, stops him. It rises in intensity, almost to an unbearable scream. He goes up and down on his toes, and rushes off around the house.*) Shhh!

Linda Willy?

There is no answer. **Linda** *waits.* **Biff** *gets up off his bed. He is still in his clothes.* **Happy** *sits up.* **Biff** *stands listening.*

Linda (*with real fear*) Willy, answer me! Willy!

There is the sound of a car starting and moving away at full speed.

Linda No!

Biff (*rushing down the stairs*) Pop!

As the car speeds off, the music crashes down in a frenzy of sound, which becomes the soft pulsation of a single cello string. **Biff** *slowly returns to his bedroom. He and* **Happy** *gravely don their jackets.* **Linda** *slowly walks out of her room. The music has developed into a dead march. The leaves of day are appearing over everything.* **Charley** *and* **Bernard**, *somberly dressed, appear and knock on the kitchen door.* **Biff** *and* **Happy** *slowly descend the stairs to the kitchen as* **Charley** *and* **Bernard** *enter. All stop a moment when* **Linda**, *in clothes of mourning, bearing a little bunch of roses, comes through the draped doorway into the kitchen. She goes to* **Charley** *and takes his arm. Now all move toward the audience, through the wall-line of the kitchen. At the limit of the apron,* **Linda** *lays down the flowers, kneels, and sits back on her heels. All stare down at the grave.*

Requiem

Charley It's getting dark, Linda.

Linda *doesn't react. She stares at the grave.*

Biff How about it, Mom? Better get some rest, heh? They'll be closing the gate soon.

Linda *makes no move. Pause.*

Happy (*deeply angered*) He had no right to do that. There was no necessity for it. We would've helped him.

Charley (*grunting*) Hmmm.

Biff Come along, Mom.

Linda Why didn't anybody come?

Charley It was a very nice funeral.

Linda But where are all the people he knew? Maybe they blame him.

Charley Naa. It's a rough world, Linda. They wouldn't blame him.

Linda I can't understand it. At this time especially. First time in thirty-five years we were just about free and clear. He only needed a little salary. He was even finished with the dentist.

Charley No man only needs a little salary.

Linda I can't understand it.

Biff There were a lot of nice days. When he'd come home from a trip; or on Sundays, making the stoop; finishing the cellar; putting on the new porch; when he built the extra bathroom; and put up the garage. You know something, Charley, there's more of him in that front stoop than in all the sales he ever made.

Charley Yeah. He was a happy man with a batch of cement.

Linda He was so wonderful with his hands.

Biff He had the wrong dreams. All, all, wrong.

Happy (*almost ready to fight* **Biff**) Don't say that!

Biff He never knew who be was.

Charley (*stopping* **Happy***'s movement and reply. To* **Biff**) Nobody dast blame this man. You don't understand: Willy was a salesman. And for a salesman, there is no rock bottom to the life. He don't put a bolt to a nut, he don't tell you the law or give you medicine. He's a man way out there in the blue, riding on a smile and a shoeshine. And when they start not smiling back—that's an earthquake. And then you get yourself a couple of spots on your hat, and you're finished. Nobody dast blame this man. A salesman is got to dream, boy. It comes with the territory.

Biff Charley, the man didn't know who he was.

Happy (*infuriated*) Don't say that!

Biff Why don't you come with me, Happy?

Happy I'm not licked that easily. I'm staying right in this city, and I'm gonna beat this racket! (*He looks at* **Biff**, *his chin set.*) The Loman Brothers!

Biff I know who I am, kid.

Happy All right, boy. I'm gonna show you and everybody else that Willy Loman did not die in vain. He had a good dream. It's the only dream you can have—to come out number-one man. He fought it out here, and this is where I'm gonna win it for him.

Biff (*with a hopeless glance at* **Happy**, *bends toward his mother*) Let's go, Mom.

Linda I'll be with you in a minute. Go on, Charley. (*He hesitates.*) I want to, just for a minute. I never had a chance to say good-by.

Charley *moves away, followed by* **Happy**. **Biff** *remains a slight distance up and left of* **Linda**. *She sits there, summoning herself. The flute begins, not far away, playing behind her speech.*

Linda Forgive me, dear. I can't cry. I don't know what it is, but I can't cry. I don't understand it. Why did you ever do that? Help me, Willy, I can't cry. It seems to me that you're just on another trip. I keep expecting you. Willy, dear, I can't cry. Why did you do it? I search and search and I search, and I can't understand it, Willy. I made the last payment on the house today. Today, dear. And there'll be nobody home. (*A sob rises in her throat.*) We're free and clear. (*Sobbing more fully, released:*) We're free. (**Biff** *comes slowly toward her.*) We're free . . . We're free . . .

Biff *lifts her to her feet and moves out up right with her in his arms.* **Linda** *sobs quietly.* **Bernard** *and* **Charley** *come together and follow them, followed by* **Happy**. *Only the music of the flute is left on the darkening stage as over the house the hard towers of the apartment buildings rise into sharp focus.*

Curtain.

Notes

Act One

1 *Requiem*. Memorial for the dead.

2 *today*. The play is intended to be set in the 1940s.

7 *Biff is a lazy bum! . . . There's one thing about Biff—he's not lazy.* One of many scenes in which Willy Loman contradicts himself. These contradictions and inconsistencies are related to Willy's deep state of denial about his own status and that of his son Biff that vacillates with fleeting moments of clarity. This interplay between dreaming and facing the truth plagues Willy throughout the play, which tinges with irony his rhetorical question to Linda: *'Why am I always being contradicted?'* (p. 8).

8 *The way they boxed us in here.* One of several references to the encroachment of surrounding apartment buildings on the Loman home in contrast to the pastoral aura invoked in Willy's daydreams of the past, signified by a leaf motif that is projected through the stage lighting.

10 *simonize*. To wax (a car).

19 *football.* Refers to American football (not soccer).

19 *Gene Tunney*. (1897–1978) World heavyweight boxing champion 1926–1928.

22 *knickers*. Trousers that go to the knees.

22 *Regents*. Regents Exams are standardized tests given to high school students in New York

27 *I'm fat. I'm very—foolish to look at, Linda.* Miller's original intention for the casting of Willy was someone small and slight like his Uncle Manny, but when 6 foot 200 pound actor Lee J. Cobb was cast, these lines were added to the play, along with Willy relaying to Linda that a fellow salesman called him a 'walrus'.

32 *let's shoot.* 'shoot' is the action of playing cards in a card game.

49 *take a fade.* Skip work.

63 *Jack Benny*. (1894–1974) A popular comedian.

66 *the New York, New Haven and Hartford.* Train line that runs from Boston to/from New York, stopping in cities in Connecticut along the way.

67 *Al Smith*. (1873–1944) Four-time governor of New York and Democratic Party candidate for president in 1928.

70 *Why must everybody conquer the world? You're well liked, and the boys love you.* This scene from Willy's memory of the past reveals insights into Linda's character and her relationship with her husband. Here she talks Willy out of pursuing business with his brother Ben in Alaska and reprimands Ben, while feeding Willy's pipe dreams and obsessive desire to be liked, revealing Linda to be more than merely a meek enabler and devoted admirer of her husband.

74 *Red Grange*. (1903–1991) American football player on Chicago Bears team.

Act Two

81 *J. P. Morgan*. (1837–1913) Wealthy and powerful American banker.

83 *hit a number.* Win money gambling.

84 *strudel*. Old-fashioned slang term for a pretty girl (comes from a pastry).

87 *no soap.* Slang for 'it didn't work out'.

88 *Dad is never so happy as when he's looking forward to something.* Happy's comment about Willy is in the context of trying to persuade Biff to lie to his father about a job opportunity with Bill Oliver and keep him hanging indefinitely, but it also points to an important motif in the play: waiting. Each member of the Loman family is depicted in liminal states of prolonged waiting, longing, dreaming and/or indecision.

90 *bullin' around*. Talking nonsense or wasting time.

100 *a sixty-one.* Sixty-five points is a passing grade.

103 *chippies*. Slang for prostitutes.

108 *on the barrelhead; gilt-edged*. Immediate cash payment (no credit extended); sure thing or safe investment.

114 *drummer*. Slang for travelling salesman.